Date Due

WRITING THE CREATIVE ARTICLE

by

Marjorie Holmes

Boston   THE WRITER, INC.   *Publishers*

Library of Congress Cataloging in Publication Data

Holmes, Marjorie, 1910–
   Writing the creative article.

   1. Authorship.   I. Title.
PN147.H64 1973   808'.066'07   73–9646
ISBN 0–87116–100–1

Printed in the United States of America

*For Jim Liston, Elliott McCleary
and Gardner Soule*

Acknowledgments

The author wishes to thank all the writers whose works have been cited as examples, and to express appreciation to the following publications for graciously granting permission to quote from them: *Better Homes and Gardens, Catholic Digest, Christian Herald, Family Circle, Family Digest, Good Housekeeping, Ladies' Home Journal, Lady's Circle, Life, McCall's, Pageant, Parents' Magazine, Petroleum Today, Reader's Digest, Rural Virginia, Today's Health, Glamour, Harper's Bazaar, Saturday Review, The Saturday Evening Post, Sports Afield, U. S. Lady, Vogue, Woman's Day.* Also, Houghton Mifflin Company, and The Seabury Press.

M. H.

Contents

Introduction
to New Edition

A teacher I had in the eighth grade (and then by a remarkable stroke of fortune, for freshman English in college) wrote the following words on one of my notebooks—words that were often to keep me going during periods of discouragement, words that were to influence my writing itself:

> You must make the most of your talent—you have been endowed with so much. I can feel joy with these paragraphs, I can feel sorrow, I am moved by their imagery. I know that if you want to badly enough, you can write beautiful things for people who ·a.ve beautiful things. There is a duty!

There is a duty. . .

Talent is a gift. You had nothing to do with receiving yours, nor I with receiving mine. But each of us has everything to do with what becomes of that talent. I am firmly convinced that each of us is given his talent for a reason; and that having talent, any talent, but particularly one for writing, imposes two responsibilities.

First: Talent must not go to waste.

What is the true cause of wasted talent? I think it's primarily a lack of that sense of responsibility or duty. Too often talent is regarded as a mere adornment, something with which to amuse yourself and dazzle your friends. That's how it seems when one is very young. I used to write long continued stories which the kids passed around in school (ending when the tablet paper ran out). I dashed off poems dedicated to everybody in sight and read aloud on all possible occasions. I even wrote my own declamatory pieces. And it was all part of a heady show-off syndrome.

Yet deep beneath all this ran a fierce compulsion: I *had* to write. Even minus an audience, into a vast notebook, late at night, I had to write. And what clinched this compulsion for me and turned it into a profession were the words: "There is a duty."

People who fail to follow up their own bright promise seem to lack this compulsion. It is much easier, of course, to regard your talent not simply as essential if awesome equipment for an important calling, but as an ornament to be kept in a drawer. You know it's there, your pretty little talent, and you can always dust it off and don it if you wish—when you're "inspired." Or delight admiring friends by doing witty news-letters for some organization or by composing the club show.

Yet you know, deep in your guts you know, you can and should be doing so much more.

The list of excuses for wasted talent is endless. But those who take their talent as a serious responsibility appraise this obstacle course and figure out their priorities: "Is it more important to attend that meeting or to get on with my article? . . . I have a doctor's appointment at three, but if I get started at nine, that still gives me five hours at the typewriter. No, subtract an hour for interruptions, and that still leaves four for writing."

When people ask how I've done it—raised four children while writing hundreds of magazine pieces and twenty books —I tell them: "I'm disciplined and I'm organized." I learned early to forego temptations and to budget time. Any house-hold has a reasonable facsimile of a schedule. I planned my writing hours to fit into it. When I lost a day to the emer-gencies that befall any family, I made it up on weekends.

My English teacher had said, *"If you want to write badly enough, you can,"* and those words, framed over my desk, often goaded me on. And how grateful, on many counts, I am. For in the end your talent does become your adornment. You make speeches, travel, appear on talk shows. But such rewards, however glittering, pale beside the significance of what has really happened. The true value of your talent has grown immeasurably. Because you respected it, were true to it and developed it, that talent now reaches far beyond you and affects many lives.

The writer's *second* responsibility is: *To use his talent for good.* Not to preach or exhort or reform necessarily, but to affirm life rather than debase it, to inspire and help and encourage. . . *"You can write beautiful things for people who crave beautiful things. . . ."* Despite the cynicism, materialism, violence and sex that seems to pervade almost every medium of communication, including the articles in many of today's magazines—despite the avalanche of products that pander to a lust for the perverse, the ugly, the decadent, there is still a vast hunger for things of the spirit, beautiful things. And the writer who is able to nourish and fill that hunger creatively and honestly is beginning to reap incredible and long overdue riches.

I am not talking about pieties and preachments, or writing that simply shuts its eyes and pretends there is no evil or sorrow in the world. But rather writing that shows the basic goodness and decency of human beings despite their trials; that celebrates compassion and love and wonder and all the other things that make life worthwhile.

I wrote in the inspirational field from the beginning. I found that facts bored me, and research took too much time away from home and typewriter. For me it was easier and more fulfilling to write creative articles born out of my own experience or observation, personal discoveries or formulas for living. And whether torn out of the very pit of suffering, or sprung from an incessant love affair with life, all were upbeat, constructive. Like Oscar Hammerstein, I found it "just as important to sing about beautiful mornings as it is to talk about slums."

Today, more than ever, people are desperate to find some

meaning and hope in life. Perhaps to compensate for their confusion, more creative articles than ever are being published. The field is wide open to any writer of good creative articles who is willing to study the markets. Religious or spiritually oriented publications are booming. And there are literally hundreds of others available, some on newsstands, some mainly by subscription. In addition to the religious, these include: Retirement, such as *Modern Maturity*. Tabloid newspapers such as *National Enquirer,* and newspaper supplements such as *Parade*. General interest magazines, sponsored by airlines, such as *The American Way;* beauty parlors, such as *Girl Talk;* hotels, such as *Holiday Inn;* car manufacturers, such as *Ford Times*. Confessions, such as *True Story*. Club or fraternal journals, such as *The Elks Magazine*. Health magazines, such as *Family Health*. Regional magazines, such as *Virginia Wildlife*. All these, plus a dizzying number of miscellaneous publications from *Grit* to *Guideposts,* from *Fate* to the prestigious *Reader's Digest,* which not only pays the most but has done more to enhance the stature of the creative article than any magazine. It publishes only the best, and it publishes so many.

Study every issue of your writers' magazines for market notes, and buy every available market guide. Using a yellow highlight pencil, mark every place where the words home, children, humor, nostalgia, self-help, etc., occur. You will find the publishing world suddenly lighting up with possibilities. Again and again you will also find the advice about style and tone exactly as given in this text: "Light and lively." "Nothing pious or preachy." "Crisp, fast-moving, with a friendly tone." Some publications offer free samples. Write and ask for them.

Furthermore, there is still room in the big slicks. My latest survey of nearly 5,000 paying markets revealed a surprise. While soundly researched fact pieces, preferably about contemporary people and events, continue to lead the field (along with sex), running a close second is the article of personal experience. Listen to *Cosmopolitan:* "Tell readers how to improve and enjoy their lives." *Family Circle:* "Human-interest stories with personal significance for readers." The individual has come into his own. If you have actually been through a divorce or lost a child or built an A-frame house, if you have had your face lifted or marched in a demonstration—if you have gone through anything large or small that will be of help or interest to other people, your account will be believed and heeded, as much if not more than if it came from a celebrity.

The types of creative article most in demand, after the personal experience, are humor, nostalgia, and inspirational. People like to laugh, and they long to escape to a past when life at least seemed to be less threatening. Above all, they are seeking answers for coping with problems now. The straight "how to get ahead" piece or "how to be happy" piece, after a lull, is staging a comeback. Due maybe to the fantastic success of such books as *I'm OK, You're OK,* and *How to Be Your Own Best Friend,* self-help articles are almost as popular as they became after Dale Carnegie's classic *How to Win Friends and Influence People* launched the trend. Anyway, editors are very open to them—*if* they are well written, really have something to say, are backed up by authority, and are soundly rooted in personal experience.

One important bonus from writing creative articles is that they are such a natural springboard for books. I know many writers whose books evolved either as a collection of their published articles or as an expanded version of one or more of their themes. My own case is not unique. It was a long apprenticeship in the magazines that led directly to my column "Love and Laughter" in the Washington *Star.* The best of these columns, plus some of the magazine sketches, became the Doubleday book *Love and Laughter;* the Hallmark book *To Treasure Our Days;* two EPM books, *As Tall as My Heart* and *Beauty in Your Own Yard;* and a just released little set of Gibson books on Faith, Love, Friends, Joy, Growth and Living.

Doubleday followed *Love and Laughter* with three books of conversational prayers: *I've Got to Talk to Somebody, God; Who am I, God?; Nobody Else Will Listen.* And a book of personal sketches and meditations, *How Can I Find You, God?* All of them are actually creative articles simply presented in a more introspective and spiritual form.

Another book, *You and I and Yesterday,* published by William Morrow, consists entirely of nostalgic articles, most of them first appearing in *Today's Health.*

At this writing, the hardcover trade sales of my books are well over two million copies. Bantam reports five million of my paperbacks in print. And book club, foreign and special editions make the total count astronomical. Add to this magazine reprints (now we are right back where we started!), and the rewards are staggering. And all because, like so many of you right now, I was once tied down with home and family, and hamstrung by an innate dread of legwork. Or maybe even more important, the things I longed to express came not from outside sources but from my own reflections, observations and convictions. The trick was in simply making them applicable to everybody else.

Inadvertently, I discovered an invaluable secret to successful writing: reader identification, and help. If you can write something that makes the reader cry out, "Hey, that's me!" and at the same time offer him hope and help, then you have a foolproof formula.

This book is an attempt to share that secret, and to help *you.*

WRITING THE CREATIVE ARTICLE

1
What Is the Creative
Article?

For the truly creative writer there is no quicker, easier, more satisfying road to paid publication than the creative article. I discovered its many blessings at the very beginning of my career. Breaking my heart over stories which might or might not sell, laboring eternally on a novel, I found that this one form never failed. I needed only to stop, write a short, bright article based on my own observations or experience to enjoy that marvelous restorative, an acceptance. The check might be miniscule or it might be impressive, but invariably it came; and mostly (though not always) on the first submission.

Sometimes, lured by someone who had a "marvelous article idea" for me, I went out and dug for facts. Sometimes the arrival of a celebrity in our small town provided a challenge and temptation. I interviewed Dale Carnegie and Margaret Bourke-White and the late famous stunt driver, Jimmy Lynch. But as I juggled home arrangements, hailed taxis, nervously waited for appointments, and trudged through plant or store or stable, I felt a curious misery growing in me. "Why am I doing this?" I demanded of myself. And later, poring over a morass of material gathered in my "research," I found that the question persisted. It was all too evident that I could have written several stay-at-home articles with half the time and trouble. Also, surprisingly, these "sure-fire" research articles

3

were often harder to place and in the end brought less than those I turned out without stirring from my typewriter.

In short, some of us are simply not journalists. We'd rather *write* than do research. And for us, when we're not involved in fiction, the best bet is what is sometimes called the self-help, art-of-living, or popular psychology piece, but there are so many variations that I prefer to shepherd them all under the comprehensive term: The Creative Article, which can be any of the following:

1. Advice
2. Personal experience
3. Vigorous protest
4. Essays about some phase of life
5. Nostalgia
6. Humor
7. Inspiration

To define terms further: The creative article is neither fact nor fiction, though it contains elements of both. It deals with human relationships. It is any article in which *ideas* are more important than facts, and whose purpose is to help, teach, amuse, move or inspire. Preferably it should do all at the same time.

A large order? Not for the person equipped to write such articles. And the advantages are many: Creative articles require almost no legwork, as I've indicated; they are less complicated than fiction; and although some editors are prejudiced against "think pieces" except from the experts, really good ones are highly salable, make magazine covers, and are snapped up for reprints.

The stay-at-home writer

This brings us to the question, "Why creative?" True, all good writing demands creative ability, whether it be a report on superhighways, supermarkets, or supermen. And the best fact articles shine with the creative personality that has deftly marshaled and meshed the facts. But the truly creative article, like fiction, emerges entirely out of the author's own vision and experience of life. And while he may (and should) support it with the testimony of others to provide some proof of what he says, the originality of his concept and his conviction predominates.

Are you the person to try it? If so, you've probably had at least a mild flirtation with fiction. You have an ear for dialogue, are fascinated by character—what makes people tick. You can dramatize, or learn to. Good articles read like stories, peppered with anecdotes or little scenes. A favored technique is the anecdotal opening, wherein the reader is hooked and lured into your subject. Some writers carry this so far it's hard for a reader to tell for a few paragraphs whether he's reading an article or a story. This I don't recommend, but the creative article writer should have imagination and the ability to compress action into a telling illustration.

Next, you probably like to give advice. People confide their troubles to you. And though your solutions may not always *work*, they sound great. You probably react first with emotion, then with logic, to both their problems and your own. (The creative article needs both.) You must be basically an optimist, in love with life, and whatever blows it deals you, you're just busting out all over with schemes for making it better: how to get along with the neighbors, your husband, or yourself; how to find beauty in the ordinary, to deal with dread, to come through hell—if not unblistered at least without third-degree burns.

Fundamentally you have to be an egotist whose ideas and experiences seem so vital that you simply must express them, if not in fiction, then in its first cousin—essays and articles which will convey your enthusiasms, your ideals, your convictions.

Finally, you should have, or be able to develop, a sense of organization, and a smooth, friendly, but never didactic style. If you can add a twist of wit, a dash of humor, so much the better. Quite apart from the value and freshness of the original ideas, it is *the way they are written* that makes such articles sell.

Similarities and variations

Back now to our original list. Obviously, the categories overlap. For instance, it would be impossible to give advice without bringing in personal experience, perhaps nostalgia, and let's hope the advice is inspiring, possibly humorous. But there are definite differences among article types:

1. The *advice* article is exactly that. It deals with the just-mentioned how-to's. A classic example that may have started the whole trend is Dale Carnegie's book, *How to Win Friends and Influence People*. Articles of this genre often use those words, actual or implied, in the title: "How to Make Home Life Happy," (how to) "Keep Your Husband in Your Arms." Or they utilize do's and don'ts in the same fashion: "Don't Be Afraid of Your Emotions," (do) "Get Rid of That Gun."

The article proper consists of firm but engaging arguments for its theme, with lifelike illustrations (or maybe just one good one). You may include a list of do's, don'ts or how-to's, or rules to follow. It helps to include a few quotes, classic or contemporary. If the idea hasn't been done to death, and if the advice is entertaining as well as sound, editors will buy it.

2. The *personal experience* article is exemplified by the "First-Person" stories in *Reader's Digest*. Drama in real life. You find them, too, in such magazines as *McCall's*; *Redbook*; *Good Housekeeping*; the fraternal journals such as *Elks, Rotarian*. In fact, almost any general circulation magazine from the confessions to the religious publications will use personal

experiences, provided they are dramatic—in the sense that they are interesting, and have something to say. Furthermore, there has been a marked change in editorial attitude over the past ten years, so that more personal experience articles are wanted, whether dramatic or not; because if you've actually been through something, you know what you're talking about—it makes for a valid theme.

The January, 1973 issue of *Reader's Digest* demonstrates personal drama: "Ordeal in the Snow." About a girl whose car flipped over in a storm and pinned her there for hours before help came. A First Person Award went to "Truce in the Forest." A German girl's moving story of how seven battle-weary boys, half German, half American, turned up at her mother's cottage and nursed each other's wounds while sharing supper on Christmas Eve. Whether your experience is epic ("I Shot Down Yamamoto"), or unique ("The Bear That Came to Dinner"), or one with which many readers can identify ("I Was Afraid to Have a Baby," "The Day My Husband Left Me," etc.), it *must* have elements of universality.

Let me illustrate from my own articles:

"Little One Late," about our postscript baby, sold promptly. Though the idea had been done (and will be again) a thousand times, I brought something fresh to it; and any woman could share that sense of shock, transformed through the curious alchemy of love into blessing. But I had a devil of a time placing the tale of how our 13-year-old caught an eight-foot, hundred-pound marlin, which he and his dad (who'd never even mounted a minnow) decided to stuff in our basement. Very funny, editors agreed, "but not enough readers go deep-sea fishing or try taxidermy." I had to tone down the incredible complications and tone up the recognition factors (father-son relationship, ingenuity) before that darned fish was landed.

3. Articles of *protest* or *controversy*. The *Speaking Out* section of *The Saturday Evening Post* was once an outstanding market, and back issues remain a gold mine of examples. Study

them, if you can, as well as current samples. There are still plenty of magazines that use this approach. You simply sound off, with fire, fervor, and some good sound logic, on something that has been bugging you: "Down With Dogs," "A Vote Against Motherhood," "Let's Keep Christmas Commercial." If you can make a lot of people react angrily, so much the better; they'll read it if only to disagree.

You'll be surprised, though, how many come out cheering. Infuriated by indecent movies, I wrote an article called, "A Mother Speaks Up for Censorship." Now "censor" is a dirty word to a lot of people; murder, mayhem, obscenity pale beside it. I fully expected to be lambasted. Instead, 90% of the deluge of letters that poured in agreed with me!

The subject under protest should, of course, be of general interest. (If you're angry at an individual, write to your diary; if the street lights in your hometown displease you, address the local paper.) And the situation should be sufficiently accepted to make your dissenting outcry extraordinary and thus worth listening to.

4. *Essays* are hard to define. Their purpose is not to advise or to protest, but to observe; to express something significant or lovely about the things we usually take for granted. You'll find them blooming like unexpected flowers in magazines that range from *The Atlantic Monthly* to *Glamour*. *Good Housekeeping* uses them fairly often, and so does *McCall's*. Sometimes as long as an article, sometimes as short as a column, they are actually sketches; if artfully done, prose poems. One I particularly liked was "The Light in the Window," by Jean Bell Mosley in *Woman's Day*. Another, Robert W. Wells' "Goodbye, My Son," from *Ladies' Home Journal*. (A father's recognition of how fleeting is childhood as he walks in the woods with his boys.)

Some of mine have been fashioned from homely, everyday phrases that speak of a way of life, a philosophy: "Mother,

I'm Home!", "Dad, I Need Some Money," "Like Mother Used to Make." Or they spring from a simple but significant object: "The Family Calendar," "Children and a Tent," "The Letter Home."

They must be succinct yet graceful; subtle yet with the point crystal clear; tender without being sentimental. They must strike a responsive chord. When they do, readers clip them and copy them and sometimes paste them in scrapbooks or carry them in wallets. At least they write and tell you so, which makes you feel good.

5. *Nostalgia.* For this you need mostly a vivid memory and a colorful style. You don't actually have to believe that the good old days were better, but you write about them with fondness and good humor. The format I use for the series is to open with a current situation (a child at the market exclaiming, "Look, Mommy, vegetables you don't even have to defrost!") and contrast it with the past (every backyard had a garden—if yours didn't, you were considered either shamefully rich or low-class). I then explore every aspect of the *one phase* of the past I'm trying to recall, and draw some conclusions: "We ate our way through summer, from the first crisp carrots to the peanuts we roasted in the bonfires of fall. No competition from Good Humor men; no adult voices urging, 'Now eat your vegetables, take your vitamins.' " And: "I wish my children could make little boats out of new-picked pods, and eat green apples, and raid a watermelon patch. . . . Since they can't, I want them to know that fruits and vegetables don't grow on the shelves of a supermarket. . . . That somewhere they are being harvested by human hands out of God's own earth and sun and sky." *

Nostalgia is back in style. In fact, it's become almost a national craze. How long this will last is anybody's guess, but in my survey I found nostalgia running close to humor and personal experience in popular demand. The major magazines, however, are "up to their calendars" in it, as one editor says;

* *Today's Health,* published by The American Medical Association

so your best bet is to try the lesser markets. Particularly regional ones, especially if you can tie your memories to the locale. Locale is great fun to write, but *don't* find it all too quaint, and don't cover too much ground.

6. *Humor,* of course, is always scarce, and editors are mad for it. But to be born with a literary funny bone is about as rare a gift as ESP. The lords of the humorous article are Art Buchwald, Russell Baker, Alan King. Among the ladies we find Erma Bombeck, Peg Bracken, Jean Kerr. If you hanker to write humor, you'd do well to study these writers; you'll laugh —and you just might learn.

Frankly, I can't tell you what makes a genuinely funny article. But I can tell you what *doesn't*—having seen so much of it in manuscript: obvious jokes and overworked puns, excessive swearing and slang, comic book posturings, situations that went out with Mack Sennett, italicized words and exclamation points. I guess humor is just that secret inner tickle that only the born humorist knows how to scratch. But if you feel that particular itch, immerse yourself in the best examples of the craft, and observe just how the writer gets his effects.

7. The *inspirational* article is a cross between essay, advice, and personal experience. It sticks to a single theme. And that theme is always something constructive, something good. A symbol is frequently employed to clarify and enhance that theme: "Bring to It the Rainbow" is the title of one by John Kord Lagemann in *Christian Herald.* Meaning "the glow that crowns an all-out effort to do any kind of job." I used a similar thought in "The Afterglow" (*Guideposts*), referring to that last lingering band of sunset that to my mother signified hope. Sometimes a memory device is utilized, as in "What Makes Courage?" by Margaret Blair Johnstone in *Reader's Digest.* (Three p's—perspective, perseverance, principle.)

The writer shares, discusses and illustrates some discovery he has made about the art of living. He may even gently offer a few suggestions as to how you may enjoy the same concept. He never preaches or dictates, he simply—well—inspires.

I think it's a good sign that you find such articles in almost every magazine. Often they're featured on the cover, or offered as reprints. The world is sex weary, war weary; people are desperately sick of crime and violence, of disease and trouble. Beneath that cynical front they long for tenderness, for decency, for hope, for some path to inner peace.

If you're truly a creative writer, you'll be able to write the creative article. In so doing you'll be helping other people, as well as yourself. Some editors call these articles "top of the head." I like to think of them as "deep of the heart."

2

The Magic of
Getting Ideas

"Where do you get your ideas?"

That question is probably asked of writers more often than any other.

Ideas, by their very nature, have a kind of magic—as if springing from some mysterious source. For there is a certain magic about all creative writing, just as there is about any art. The writer or artist must first possess that magic lamp—talent —capable of producing the genie of ideas. The genie may come unsought, but more often he appears with his rich treasure because the possessor of the lamp (the writer or artist) has learned how to summon him.

Thus, to that original question the experienced writer can only reply, "Where do you *stop* getting ideas?" Having trained himself to be aware, and to recognize ideas, his problem is far less one of lack than of selection. Almost literally there is no person, situation, emotion or experience, no remark whether witty or mundane, even no object however humble that couldn't generate for him an idea, or a dozen, for a creative article.

Once a writer has achieved this happy state, he may find it hard to remember that the simple business of finding something to write about is often a problem to the beginner. Yet if he's honest he will recall a time when he too felt the awful burning of his special lamp, yet seemed powerless to release the genie who would produce ideas. How, then, did he free the genie? *By sitting down and writing.*

Don't wait, write

The first step any writer takes toward the "magic" that seems to come with professionalism is simply to sit down and write. The idea that launches him may be good, bad, or indifferent; but the only way to move on toward other, perhaps better, ideas is to get rid of the one you have.

For many people this is extremely difficult. They procrastinate for fear that, having used up that one precious idea, there will be nothing else to take its place. Everywhere I go I meet someone who has "an idea" for an article or story. Often he's had it for years. He asks about how to handle it; he wonders if he should copyright it in case an editor tries to steal it. Very often he begs the professional writer to write it for him (for half the proceeds) in order to spare himself the ordeal of coping with it alone, and thereafter becoming bereft of ideas.

Such one-idea specialists never become writers. They don't even qualify for kindergarten in the long, hard school of writing—which requires them to establish regular working habits. Perhaps this is just as well, for they are motivated more by the persistent wish to be published than by the burning need to write. The truly creative person (and the only one who should tackle either the creative article or fiction) *has* to write, whether or not he seems to have anything to write about. He is drawn to his desk almost against his will. He may think of excuses to postpone the misery of perhaps finding he has no ideas, but in the end he submits; he begins to discipline himself to his daily stint.

Once this happens, a remarkable thing occurs: Ideas come. And ideas were not meant to be hoarded. Like the cow that must be milked, or the flowers that must be picked in order to continue blooming, ideas must be spent. And the more prodigal you are with your thoughts, the more enriched your imagination and creative skills become. In the throes of one article or story, you often find so many new ideas popping up, clamoring for attention that you can hardly wait to finish and go on with them.

Recognizing ideas

Too many would-be writers grope blindly for ideas, unable to recognize the ones that skitter all around them.

After my first lecture in a recent course, a student sent me a note in desperation. She had a consuming longing to write, and a brisk, deft style—but she claimed, "I don't know what to write about. I am absolutely devoid of ideas."

One day, having coffee with her after class, I discovered that she was English, had a radiant personality, and a bubbling fund of hilarious anecdotes from her travels all over the world. Her husband was in the diplomatic corps. She deplored the constant rounds of entertaining, the constant uprooting of herself and children. As she spoke, I kept interrupting with, "There's an idea!" . . . The false faces people wear to cocktail parties. How to inure yourself to such affairs when you don't feel like going. The wild and wonderful comparisons between British and American schools. How to get along with a husband whose career is travel when you long only to settle down with a pot of tea and a good book.

Nothing to write about? She was loaded! Failing to recognize the wealth of material in her own experience, she had spent none of it; hence, her imagination failed to function constructively. She had simply never taken a detached professional look at herself. Thus she had not gleaned any *angle of interpretation,* which is, actually, all that any article idea is.

On the other hand, there are people who have traveled extensively and perhaps lived abundantly who feel that just because they have all this "wonderful material" they are qualified to write. Alas, they are often mistaken—because they never quite hit upon that cogent *angle of interpretation,* which is, I repeat, the crux of the creative article idea.

It is not enough simply to relate your observations or experiences; you, the author, must point and shape them to some fresh lesson or purpose. To learn to do this, you must 1) be constantly alert to the article material in your own life; 2) practice writing about it; 3) read creative articles; 4) train your mind.

Train the mind—subconscious and conscious

That marvelous instrument, the mind, has for all practical, useful purposes, two layers—the conscious and the subconscious (or, if you prefer, the *unconscious*). The writer learns to use both in the begetting of ideas.

Let's consider first the subconscious—that layer of mind that suddenly awakens, brimming with thoughts when the rest of you wants to sleep. If you're worried, it thrashes about incessantly, seeking solutions. If you've had a stimulating experience, the subconscious keeps replaying it. In short, its activity is always triggered by a thought, event, experience, person. Thus, if you really want a good idea, or some fortifying ones for the piece you're working on, try this: Simply read several good articles in similar vein before settling down. Or merely read a number of titles! Then close your eyes and relax, while the ideas come zooming in.

It's a very old trick which I learned from a college art teacher who advised us to look at books of design or paintings before going to bed: "You'll be surprised at how many new, underivative yet excellent pictures will leap from your own subconscious." This was true; it worked, and has been working for me ever since. Other writers verify this; some even keep couches in their studies for the purpose. (I used to, but mine always got so covered up with papers I could never find it.)

The first creative article I ever wrote was the result of reading through a single issue of *Your Life*, a magazine with articles giving formulas for better living, written in a friendly, honest and engaging style. When I put down that first issue and turned out the lights, my mind presented me with a whole flock of thoughts. One of them was so insistent I got up and began to write. Before morning I had finished a 1500-word piece, "You Can Be Too Good a Sport," which was promptly bought. This is also a demonstration of that well-known law: *Write the kind of thing you read.* The advice is good for more than one reason. If you read the magazines you want to write for, you are learning to slant toward a definite market. And meanwhile, your subconscious is absorbing a certain tone and rhythm of writing, and storing up that curious power that in turn creates your own ideas.

Once you have established the writing habit, the clamor of creative ideas will not be limited to the time you spend at the typewriter. Your subconscious will present them to you while you are doing things totally unrelated to writing—shingling the roof, riding on a subway, scrubbing the floor. Much as I deplore time-consuming housework, it is sometimes an advantage to have to clean up the kitchen or vacuum before getting to my study. The mind has to occupy itself with something, and more often than not, it ponders the complexities of personal relationships, situations with family or neighbors, scraps of dialogue, little scenes that reveal human nature, memories. All the teeming stuff of the creative article. And out of it will suddenly come winging a phrase, a slant, frequently a title that itself proposes or states the premise of a likely piece. Whatever you are occupied with, if you write regularly, your subconscious will keep you tuned and focused toward more writing, productive writing, by constantly feeding you ideas. It will become your best ally.

There are also methods you can consciously apply and definite places you can look for ideas. Let's consider just one. Train your mind *consciously* to get to work on your next writing project even as you ride that subway, shingle that roof, or scrub that floor. Direct it toward the basic idea, and let it start sorting and assembling the peripheral ideas that will appear. This kind of mental discipline is invaluable. It will spare you the frustration that comes with delays and save you time. You will find that a great deal has been accomplished by the time you reach your desk.

Keep a notebook

Conscious, subconscious, or unconscious—wherever they come from, ideas aren't much use unless you put them down. In addition to the habit of writing regularly, the second most valuable habit any writer can have is: Keeping a notebook.

By this I mean any form in which you set down these ideas while they are fresh. It can be a notepad carried in your pocket; it can be a looseleaf journal. It can even be any scrap of paper on which you scribble, providing you later transpose your notes into something legible in a notebook, card file, or a Manila folder.

After years of using the looseleaf journal method, I have come around to the folder. In this way, every new idea that seems worthy of a separate article can be titled, if only tentatively, and alphabetically filed. Every time I get a bright thought that might be worked into the article, it too can be roughly caught and tucked into the same folder. There, also, can be assembled any supplementary material such as quotes, pertinent anecdotes, clipped articles or references which might be useful.

For the new writer, the major value in keeping a notebook is to get him into the habit of writing ideas down—not only for the value of an individual idea, but for the greater benefit of generating new ideas. Even though he may not use all of them, his awareness is intensified, like a person who never notices coins or stamps or first editions until he starts to collect them —then he suddenly sees them everywhere.

Furthermore, the ideas begin to have value in themselves.

While the writer can't use all of them, and probably won't sell all the articles he produces, the larger his fund of initial ideas the better his chances are. *lasting one day only*

But ideas are ephemeral things, likely to disappear. Whenever or wherever one occurs to you—don't wait, stop whatever you're doing and write it down. Tomorrow morning, or even an hour from now may be too late. Even if you do have a recollection of what it was all about, the essence of it, fresh and cogent and neatly phrased, may be gone. Fill your notebook with ideas now!

Five sources of creative article ideas

Suppose ideas don't simply come raining down as a reward for both your diligent labors and your mental alertness. Are there places where you can look for them? Indeed there are:

1. Newspapers

People who write fact articles constantly scan newspapers for stories of people, places and projects that they can *investigate* and expand. The creative article writer should read his newspapers with his senses attuned to the *psychology* back of the news. When a presumably model citizen absconds with the bank funds and the wife of his best friend, the creative writer asks "What if?" (What if—the man's own wife was indifferent? socially ambitious? What if—lots of men are secretly overcoming similar temptations? Lack of communication plays a part? It's a mistake for couples to see too much of each other?) By using the old dependable what-if technique, just as in fiction, you can unleash a flood of ideas.

More obvious newspaper sources are letters written to the advice columns, and the advice given by the columnists. I read one today where a woman complained of her husband's habit of taking long (loud) naps on the living room sofa instead of his own bed where he wouldn't disrupt the household. The columnist said that no one in any family should be allowed to be so inconsiderate; that to tolerate such behavior was to encourage it in the children. Now there's an idea for somebody.

2. Conversations

Tune in on other people's conversations, and your own. Listen to what people are saying at parties, on buses and trains—eavesdrop. Once, sitting behind a mother and her long-haired son, I heard him threaten: "O.K. If I can't get a motorcycle, I'll get married." Wow! Where could you find a funnier, more flagrant line to launch an article on any of the following: The gimme-kid society. The scared-parent syndrome. What's happened to marriage values? (Matrimony versus motor bike.)

Your own conversations may be even better; they are so revealing, not only of other people's attitudes, but yours. The saying, "How do I know what I think till I hear what I have to say?" is true! Get together with someone who sparks your mental forces, and you may be amazed at what brilliant ideas you spout—concepts which lie slumbering unsuspected until they are awakened by the presence of this other personality. The creative writer needs at least a few creative friends. They don't have to be writers themselves, but people who do have good minds and can be articulate. The value is twofold: A bright friend has bright ideas which he is usually delighted for you to use. Even better, his brightness fans yours.

But don't make the mistake of refusing to "waste time" on ordinary people—those who may not scintillate, but who often have a vast fund of common sense. Listen to your neighbors, to cab drivers, hairdressers, repair men, domestics. Draw them out; often their experiences are impressive, their philosophy profound. I do this constantly, and out of these "dialogues in everyday living," as I call them, have come countless articles and columns.

But again, none of this will be of benefit unless you *keep that notebook*. Hasten to the typewriter and recap the conversation as accurately as you can. You probably won't use it in toto when it comes to the actual article, but it is important to catch the essence of what was said, and then shape and sharpen it to your purpose. It will have given you what you need—the vital idea.

3. Your family

Your children. Your marriage. Your relatives.

No writer who has children should ever lack for ideas. The problems of parenthood are legion, and the ways to solve them limitless. Whether you treat the complexities of rearing children humorously or seriously, the number and variety of possibilities—from the time you hold your first baby in your arms until you comb the rice out of your hair after the last one's wedding, and even beyond—should keep you stocked with ideas. (This field is so rich with possibilities for creative articles that it will be discussed fully in a separate chapter.)

Marriage is another subject so important to the creative article writer that techniques of dealing with it will be discussed later. If yours is the ideal union, you can write what's good about it, and how come. The slant will be refreshing. If, as is more likely, you've noticed a few flaws in your own or other couples' marriages, the defects will provide the meat of many an article, serious or humorous, depending upon the style you bring to it.

As for relatives! Here ideas grow as numerous as leaves on the family tree. Brothers, sisters, cousins, and colorful maiden aunts; parents and grandparents. Amusing or inspiring tales and truths drawn from members of your clan. Among books based on these lively goldmines we think instantly of *Auntie Mame, Mama's Bank Account, Grandma Called It Carnal,* and more recently, Marion Benasutti's *No Steady Job for Papa* or

Sam Levenson's *Everything but Money*. And articles on similar subjects appear in magazines like *Reader's Digest* as "My Most Unforgettable Character," and in countless other publications.

4. Yourself

Obviously, the best source of ideas for the creative article writer is *himself*. Your reaction to the human condition, and suggestions for improving it (advice). Your righteous indignation (protest). Your spiritual growth (inspirational essay). Your adventures, simple or dramatic (personal experience). Your memories (nostalgia, or the reflective sketch). The things that make you laugh (humor).

This does not mean that the pronoun "I" will pepper your articles; it must be used judiciously. But since yours is the viewpoint and yours the voice, you are the most vital source of material you can have.

5. The articles you write

In the body of every article you write lurk the seeds of several more. Watch for them. These other article ideas lie in the material you may have to discard because it throws the basic argument out of focus or makes the article too long. Or you may find them by reversing the idea you have just written.

To illustrate: In writing an article on communication ("How to Talk to the Person You Married"), I originally included a number of common listening faults. The list was deemed too negative, and cut by the editors. Hating to let anything go to waste and still feeling I had not exhausted the subject (also still hearing the plaint, "He never tells me anything"), I blew that list up into another article which appeared as "Why Men Don't Talk to Their Wives." Then, bubbling with counter-arguments (you have to see both sides of any question), I wrote another piece, "Why Women Can't Talk to Their Husbands."

Again, writing an article about family finances ("What Is Your Paycheck Doing to Your Marriage?"), I was teased onto a tangent on working wives—a whole subject in itself. Out came that material to become the basic idea for "Whose Money Is It When Women Work?"

If you have a truly creative mind, you will always find more to be said on any subject than there is space for. Write fully, then glean and winnow until you have a tight, strong article that says only one thing and says it well. But save all those peripheral ideas; the best ones can be turned into articles that may outshine the one from which they sprang.

As I have indicated, one major reason the beginner is often stymied for ideas is that he doesn't know what to do with the ones he has! And usually the reason the writer does not know is that he hasn't organized his life around the business of writing. Herein lies the value of writers' magazines, courses, and classes and conferences with professionals, books on technique and marketing. Any and all sources of stimulus and information that will not only goad him into writing regularly but show him how to develop an idea into something salable, then direct him where and how to go about selling the finished product, are valuable.

Read everything you can about the business of writing, just as you must read the magazines you want to write for. Get the feel and flow of it into your subconscious as well. Above all, write! The more you write, the more fiercely will burn that special lamp of your talent, and the more eager its genie will be to serve you, springing up at every turn, snatching ideas from the air and offering them to you in exciting new forms. Or, should he slumber, you'll have so mastered the magic of the lamp that you can summon him up at will.

3

The Five Fundamentals

The five fundamentals of a good creative article are:

1) a provocative idea
2) an appropriate style
3) a smooth, sound structure
4) pertinent, effective anecdotes
5) a forceful summary or conclusion

What makes an idea provocative?

The idea (and the way it is presented) *is* the creative article. Not facts, remember, no matter how wisely or well arranged: Ideas! Having established this, and explored the whole vast idea warehouse of living, let's be more specific: What constitutes a good creative article idea?

I believe its two most important elements are these: *Recognition* and *Surprise*.

To the reader, the article's fundamental concept may be quite familiar, an old friend with whom he feels at ease, with whom he can identify; they speak a common language. Yet one reason he enjoys this friend is that the friend is never dull; he comes out with bright, new slants on things. "I never thought of it that way before," the reader reacts. Or he may violently disagree—"No, absolutely not, you're wrong." This is the secret of the successful idea. It offers insight into an age-old situation or problem; and whether the reader applauds or objects, he is never bored, because the topic has also given him this element of freshness and surprise.

There is, of course, nothing new under the sun. The good idea is any idea that makes the old *seem* new. It never belabors the obvious ("Mothers Should Be Good Examples," or "Happiness Is Important to the Home") but brings to the obvious an *angle of interpretation* that is uniquely worth exploring: A mother who strains too hard to set a good example may become a martinet . . . or lose her own identity. . . . Or the approach might be: "Three Little Mirrors—of Mom" or possibly, "The Toughest Job of Parenthood." The second subject (*homes should be happy*) was saved from a didactic obviousness by a straightforward approach: "How to Keep Home Life Happy." I did this in an article which accepted the obvious—O.K.; so happiness *is* important, now what do we do about it? And while the piece would win no prizes for originality, in hitting the subject head-on and offering some *specifics,* it overcame the obvious and sounded fresh.

Or let's take a subject as commonplace as the paying of compliments. By poking fun at her own failings, and telling how she adores people who will lie if necessary to tell her she's witty and beautiful, Hildegarde Dolson produced a lively, amusing piece, "I Love a Nice Liar," for *McCall's.*

Arthur Gordon uses the same subject for a lovely, thoughtful article for *Woman's Day,* "How Wonderful You Are." But what sparked his idea and furnished his basic anecdote was his coming across some old letters and reading the simple honest tributes people paid to each other in Civil War days. By using *contrast* with today's self-protective detachment, and some excellent illustrations, he established an obvious, yet richly rewarding premise: "To be manifestly loved, to be openly admired, are human needs as basic as breathing. Why, then, wanting them so much ourselves, do we deny them so often to others?"

Surprise comes from taking the opposite side of a common

stand. ("Don't Pay Me Compliments—Fix the Furnace!" "Tension Is Good for You.") The result may be an article of fervent protest, or it may evolve as a gay but sensible essay on any personal quirk, dream or conviction. For instance, Rube Goldberg's "Are You Afflicted with Promptitis?" with the subtitle, "Man's Deadliest Disease":

> There is a little instrument that governs my every move. . . . The watch that is strapped to my wrist never relaxes its leathery grip as it hurries me from place to place, only to find that the other fellow is not there. Nobody seems to know the time but me.

And how charmingly he describes his anguished waiting for plays to start, his turn at the barber's, friends who don't show:

> Some people steal. Others kiss cows. . . . We look at clocks. We are incurable. We are doomed to be on time for the rest of our lives.

First published in the Thirties, it reappeared in *Pageant* recently. Notice that it is just as fresh and "timely" as when the famous humorist originally despaired of his foible.

Another, that not only gives us surprise but sheer amazement, is "Be the First on Your Block to Own a Ton of Steel," by Marvin Kitman (*The Saturday Evening Post*). Straight humor, out of personal experience. Cogitating the steel market, the author notices that a small company is bucking the big ones, and decides to support it by buying *one* ton of steel, to be delivered. The complications for the firm, the family, and the neighborhood are hilarious.

It was a terrific idea and the author played it to the hilt. Naturally not everybody gets (or could handle) such a way-out idea. But don't be too quick to dismiss that far-fetched scheme that hits you as you wait for the traffic light to change. Remember the *what-if?* technique. What if you acted on the seemingly incredible impulse? What effect would it have on your wife, the city, mankind? What cogent message, serious or light, would it bring? We are all Mr. or Mrs. Mittys, and the seemingly fantastic is often an echo of our own secret dreams.

Never strain for the unusual, however—the strain will show. The best ideas are generally those that emerge from the simple everyday stuff of our own existence. The more you write the more you will be able to recognize that quality of something special, something unique that shines from the ordinary, and makes you cry out, "Hey, that's it. That's a good idea!"

An appropriate style

What sells the creative article is the idea and *the way it is presented*. This means both structure and style. For now let's consider just two aspects of the style: It must be clear and readable, never obscure or dryly pedantic. And it must be appropriate, both to subject matter and the author's approach.

While the light touch may be brought to most subjects, there are some where it would be fatal to be funny—death, for instance, except for rare exceptions. I once saw a student manuscript called "Great Aunt Annie's Funeral." Now had the author's *approach* been even moderately respectful, a mild sort of humor could have tastefully emerged from the gathering of a warring clan at the bier of an eccentric. Instead, the approach was slapstick, one long sick joke at the expense of a good woman and grieving people. I suppose this sort of thing could be done for, say, a funeral director's journal ("A Funny Thing Happened on the Way to the Funeral," maybe); but for general readership a flip style about a serious matter like death is wrong. (Fiction, of course, can go whole-hog. Even a fact book like Jessica Mitford's *The American Way of Death* had some highly humorous moments, but they emerged as an inevitable by-product of some of the actual situations, not because her style was consciously comic.)

An airy style would have also been woefully inappropriate for "Our Child Was Molested," an unsigned *Good Housekeeping* article. Or one I wrote for *Better Homes and Gardens*— "Protect Your Child from Sex Offenders." It opened with an anecdote—a child skipping around the church corner to play with the rector's children, and her obedient phone call less than five minutes later when she arrived. It proceeded to tell why these and other precautions were taken—all in a conversational style—never grim but certainly never amusing.

The style Hildegarde Dolson uses in "I Love a Nice Liar" is appropriate because her *approach* to the subject of compliments is so gaily unique; she is really kidding herself. Arthur Gordon's style in "How Wonderful You Are," on the other hand, is suitably earnest and tender. It would have been all wrong for him to try to be clever about letters filled with genuine sentiment and sense, or about the serious point he was making: People do crave and respond to sincere appreciation.

Articles of protest and controversy call for their own salty, sometimes brittle, sometimes funny, but always forceful style, while such articles as those by Elizabeth Bowen or Victoria Lincoln, about leisure and graceful customs and the awakening mind, call for a flowing style that would be totally out of place in, say, *Nation's Business*.

As you read, note how writers adapt their style to their material. And as you write, make sure that the style you are using is truly in harmony with the material you have chosen, and your own approach to it.

A smooth, sound structure

The basic idea which launches the article and permeates it must be made very clear by discussion, and illustrated, usually by anecdote. The manner in which this material is organized is its structure or form. The well-written article, like the well-written short story, reads so easily and smoothly that it is often difficult to realize that the form is there.

Sometimes we do find articles which seem to ramble and backtrack unnecessarily, yet make their point and make it well. O.K., fine. The idea may itself be so vital, the writing style so impressive that the structure can pretty much go hang; it will still come out all right. Enjoy these pieces, but don't be misled by them. Most creative articles follow certain patterns of organization (as you will be shown), not because anybody made a rule about it, but simply because they are more effective that way.

Anecdotes

Anecdotes are simply little stories that demonstrate the writer's point and make his message clear.

The idea is the heart or soul of the article. Its structure is its body. Its style may be considered its personality. But it is the anecdotes which activate the creative article, make it live.

In the personal experience article, there may be only one major anecdote, one single story, but this major event, incident or situation may be led up to, fortified and interpreted by several minor episodes or incidents.

The inspirational sketch is another type in which a single anecdote, often seemingly slight, may be given total focus. In most articles, however, particularly those of advice or discussion, a number of anecdotes are used. Seldom fewer than three or more than six. I have counted as many as nine on occasion, but six is an average for articles running from 1500 to 2500 words.

Where do you get your anecdotes? Well, like ideas, you get them from life itself. Friends, relatives, everybody in your entire sphere provide examples of practically anything you care to discuss. Or they continually furnish you with anecdotes about other people. At the coffee klatch, bridge table, cocktail party, church, office or P. T. A., what do people constantly discuss? People! Why? Mainly, to express their own views in relation to a situation:

"She's taken a job and Bill's furious, he wants her to stay home and look after the baby, and I don't blame him—when they wait that long for a child, then put it in a day nursery—"

"No, I hear the grandmother's coming to look after it. But boy, will that be a mistake! I'd never have an in-law in my house again, I tried it—"

"Why, my husband's mother lives with us and we get along beautifully—I don't know what we'd do without her."

Thus out of the anecdote about one person spring anecdotes from the experiences of others, and all to prove or disprove an attitude or conviction.

Or children bring you their tales from camp and club and school—stories wacky and wild and wonderful, pertinent or pathetic; some so revealing of human truth that you hasten to your notebook to set them down. Many are simply absorbed, deposited without your actually knowing it into your mental bank account from which one day, suddenly, you will make a quick and apt withdrawal.

Frequently the anecdotes must be blown up, or toned down, altered to suit our purpose; or we invent others that will. This is just as legitimate in the creative article as it is in fiction, where the author's finest characters are composites of many people. The ultimate result seems and sounds even more true because the author has trained the sharp lens of his camera upon some basic essential common to most people.

It is sometimes better to invent people and incidents anyway, so they can't recognize themselves. Don't use your boss or your next-door neighbor to illustrate negative characteristics—at least not until you've moved far away, and even then it's best to use "disguises." Naturally you'd never use anyone's real name or even initials, with these exceptions: articles of family reminiscence where the reference is complimentary; or anecdotes of famous people.

Anecdotes drawn from the lives of eminent people are a great boon to the creative article. They lend stature and authority to the point you are trying to make.

But don't make the mistake of using stock anecdotes about famous historical figures, like Ben Franklin and his kite, Washington and the cherry tree, etc. Look through biographies and

autobiographies, diaries, books of old letters to find new facts
and stories about famous figures you may be able to use to illustrate your point. Or try to find less well-known (but not
obscure) personalities to use as examples. Also, read the gossip
columnists and the speeches and articles by and about contemporary leaders. Often during political campaigns little-
known facts about candidates are brought out. Anecdotes
should never be clichés.

How do we identify the principals in other anecdotes? Sometimes they can be christened, just as in fiction—Jerry Faver-
sham, Mrs. Johnson, Father O'Boyle. (In humor you can work
some wonderfully funny effects with names.) Or you can simply
fall back on "My friend Jane." Names like "Jane B." or "Oscar
R." are in disfavor—they smack somehow of the coy or phony.
Perhaps the best device is simply to identify by occupation,
profession, or group: "A college professor tells me—," "A
young housewife down the street—," "Our daughter's English
teacher—," "A pretty girl just back from the Peace Corps—"

Showing the kind of people they are, and what they do,
serves the double purpose of making their observations more
valid. Quote freely; let *them* tell their stories. In the interest of
brevity, simply condense their experiences: "I knew a brilliant
woman lawyer who had put four children through college—
'without ever really knowing them,' she told me. 'I was always
in court or consulting with a client, when often they needed to
consult me even more desperately.' "

Dialogue in the creative article is important. And, as in fiction, it should do these things: Characterize, advance the
movement, give the reader information. In the creative article,
it must do one thing more: *Prove the point.* A sentence, even a
fragment of conversation, is often the capsule of the message:
"I wish I knew my children better—" . . . "Don't be afraid to
be friendly," Grandpa always said—"everybody's really kin-
folk—" . . . "Don't wait too long to go after what you want,"
the professor warned.

Whatever the article type, the dialogue should be succinct
and telling. It should be used in the anecdote for a definite pur-

pose: to characterize the individual and underscore the circumstances which are being used to illustrate the theme.

The summary or conclusion

Some articles just stop, leaving the reader to draw his own conclusions; articles can be very effective that way. Most articles, however, summarize what has been said. A good article should: "Tell 'em what you're going to tell 'em. Tell 'em. Then tell 'em what you've told 'em."

This "tell 'em what you've told 'em" is the packaging of the theme. In the advice article, a good way to do this is to cite and clarify the various points you have made under rules or suggestions, listed numerically: For instance: 1. Decide what you most want to do in life. 2. Train for it. 3. Go where the opportunities are.

The final point can be your final statement. Or you can go a step farther and "tie a bow on the package," by making one last conclusive statement, shining and memorable, you hope. This is just one of those extras that help an article to sell.

4

Three Ways to Put an Article Together

The best way to make a dress or to build a boat or a house is to follow a pattern or a blueprint. And very few cooks can imagine working without recipes. True, creative people can and do fashion their own patterns and recipes all the time, or they take tested ones and bring variations to them.

Similarly, in writing certain formulas are used (despite a lot of breast-beating and saying oh, no, we shouldn't) simply because they have proved effective. Madeleine L'Engle expressed it well in a recent Authors Guild *Bulletin:* "Neither you nor I can teach anybody to write. We can, however, point out that in all great writing there are certain things the masters always do, and there are certain things they never do, and we can learn from these."

The anecdote-and-discussion form of creative article is probably the most *natural* form of human discourse; it is also one of the most ancient. The Bible is filled with examples of truth vividly demonstrated through incidents in the lives of people. The effective use of this form is particularly apparent in the New Testament where we find Christ teaching and preaching in parables. He would first state his premise and then prove its validity by means of a story to which his listeners could relate. And he drew the substance of these parables from the common fund of their experience—fishing, farming, paying taxes. All his analogies and even most of his metaphors were easily recognizable to his listeners, yet succinct and often startling.

In our own experiences today, it is almost impossible to have any exchange of ideas about human relationships without following a similar form. Listen to almost any discussion about almost any subject of common interest:

"I don't believe in these college marriages, and I'll tell you why. My daughter (or neighbor, son, or nephew) went through it—" And a little story is told to illustrate the speaker's conviction.

Meanwhile, the other person is waiting to chime in with *his* concepts: "You're right. Take my niece—" Or perhaps, "I don't think so at all. Fred and I were only freshmen; nobody thought it would work, but it was very stabilizing for us both, we really learned to cooperate—"

In the previous chapter I showed how such conversation often provides the writer with usable anecdotes. Here, I want simply to point out that conversation follows an uncontrived, almost inevitable form. The progression is logical and natural. Perhaps that is why the intuitive or natural writer, or the experienced one, so often uses dialogue without even thinking about it. But the novice, not yet attuned to the fact that all writing should emerge and fall *naturally* into its most logical form, freezes up before his material. He struggles to "write an article," self-consciously putting in everything he can think of about his subject in an unnatural and literary manner. The result is often pedantic, chaotic, or both.

This, of course, is not to say that the creative article is composed of scraps of dialogue. It simply follows a similar basic framework.

Here are two of these patterns, plus suggestions for a third:

PATTERN ONE

1. The opening: Begin with straight statement of your theme, followed by an illustrative anecdote or two

Or

Begin with one or two illustrative anecdotes followed by a statement of your theme

2. Anticipate the opposition. (This can be done in the very opening, or later in the article.)

3. Enlarge upon the first anecdote, and/or

4. Use other anecdotes that further illustrate your theme

5. Link illustrations together by discussion of this theme

6. In an article of advice, real or implied, conclude with specific suggestions, sometimes enumerated

7. Summarize with a final statement or paragraph which re-emphasizes the theme

PATTERN TWO

1. The opening: Start out with a few paragraphs which discuss your theme; or start with one good anecdote

2. Anticipate your opposition

3. Lead into specific points or suggestions: 1. 2. 3., enlarging upon each one as you go, and:

4. Use anecdotes and/or discuss each as you proceed

5. Summarize briefly, or simply stop

PATTERN THREE
(your own)

If you have sufficient imagination, originality, a sense of pace and logic, you can wander as far from these two suggested frameworks as you please. You can invent or utilize other forms: the letter, the diary, the dream, the dialogue. Or you can present the material in your own way, cutting out anything that is extraneous; a readable though unstructured form quite likely will evolve.

Patterns One and Two apply primarily to the article of advice or of controversy. By analyzing such articles in the magazines, you will quickly see how continually these two formulas are used.

Pattern Three applies mostly to articles of reminiscence, personal experience, humor, or the short inspirational essay. These are categories for which there are no dependable formulas, since they depend so much upon style and tone.

Openings

The opening is one of the most important elements in the article, because it must capture the reader's interest. Here are some examples of the straight *statement* opening:

> Marriage was meant to be enjoyed. Yet the carefree side of marriage is often one of the first fond dreams to go by the board. (One of my articles in *Better Homes and Gardens*.)

> There is a wonderful afterglow of pleasure that accompanies every act of truly tactful giving. It's that blissful state that helps us forget all our misgivings. ("The Act of Giving," by Dorothy Doty, *Christian Herald*.)

> Few people set out deliberately to miss the wonder and richness of living, but it is treacherously easy to do. ("Never Say Never," by Michael Drury, *Glamour*)

> Never before have parents been forced to turn their children into a society not only teeming with temptations, but with outright propaganda for yielding to them. ("What Parents Can Do About Obscenity," a piece I did for *Family Digest*.)

These openings tackle the subject head on. They inform the reader what this article is going to be all about. The sentences are reasonably short, and there is a certainty even in the rhythms. In each instance the theme is fleshed out with a few more sentences to give it body and substance. Then follows the first proof by means of an illustrative anecdote.

In the marriage article:

> One of the most congenial pairs of our acquaintance were the Vales. Together they had built a summer cottage, even built their own swimming pool where friends flocked. Winters they entertained every other Saturday night, and on alternate ones went out. Yet, Mrs. Vale told me, the first ten years of their marriage, they had almost no friends, no fun. (Note contrast.)

In the article on giving:

> I particularly became aware of this recently when a friend gave me a little trinket. My genuine appreciation must have given her

an extra amount of happiness, for her face suddenly flushed and her smile was one of obvious delight.

In "Never Say Never":

I know a brilliant woman who has led a fascinating and rewarding life, and once I asked her if she could select the single most important lesson she had learned. She was silent a moment, then said, "Yes. That all the things you think can never happen, will happen. And that all the things you think you'll never do, you probably will do."

In "What Parents Can Do About Obscenity":

What can parents do about it? We can at least keep it out of our homes. "Throw those records out!" a dad we know ordered his son. "Your mother and I wouldn't let you eat garbage, and we won't allow you to subject yourself or the rest of the family to such stuff . . ."
And on the larger front, parents can protest . . . A friend of ours, a doctor's wife, relates her indignation at the words of one hit. . . . "I called the station and read the words of this song to the manager. . . . He seemed genuinely shocked."

Now any of these articles *could* have opened just as well with the anecdote (or other dramatic proof) itself. Reread them as if they were article openings, and you will see how easily they could have been so transposed. The author's decision to state his thesis and discuss it a bit first was merely a matter of his own feeling toward his material. It simply came out better for him that way.

Putting the anecdote first, however, is very much in favor. It makes the article open like a little story. It hooks the reader's interest because it deals with people. Once he is intrigued by this example or quotation from life, he is ready for the basic idea. He will listen while the author enlarges that idea, emphasizes it and illustrates it further.

Here are some examples of anecdotal openings, which are followed by their themes:

When I was a little girl in the parsonage, the doors of home stood wide to the world, or so it seemed to me, and people streamed in by the scores. . . . One day the caller was a girl. . . . She wore scuffed shoes, red with the clay dust of our Nova Scotia county, a battered tan sweater and an old plaid skirt, and her lipstick was too bright for her tired face. . . . (Note the color and character touches.)

An hour later she reappeared on the doorstep with my mother. . . . "Sure was a long way," she said. "But I don't care. I had to talk to somebody—"

Ardis Whitman, in her article, "Let Us Speak to One Another" (*Woman's Day*), now clearly states her theme:

Psychologists and psychiatrists tell us that many people will go to such lengths and more just to be heard and understood.

One of my own early articles, "It Takes A Little Nerve", began like this:

As a child, my mother never particularly cared to have us play with Judy because, she said, "She's got such a lot of nerve. . . ."

The theme, immediately following that opening anecdote: "I've come to believe since, however, that a dash of Judy's nerve would have been good for the shyly squelched rest of us; that often fools who rush in where angels fear to flutter *get places angels don't, and have a better time*."

Another of my articles which appeared as "How Much Sentiment at Your House?" in *Ladies' Home Journal* began:

"Oh, but he's just a baby," a friend blithely dismissed our little guy's birthday, in urging us to attend a party the other day, "he won't know the difference if you're not there."

"No, but I will," I said, "and so will the other children. He's got to have a candle and a cake and pictures to prove it, even if he is only a year old." *Because we believe in sentiment for children.* We consider it as important to them as spinach or Sunday school." (Note specifics).

Anticipate the opposition

Quite obviously articles of protest would not be written if a lot of people didn't already believe otherwise. And it's hard to

conceive of any opinion worthy of any discussion that would not
have its exceptions, and its dissenters. Some writers may not
even mention this; some may leave it until the end of the
article. But I think it is an important and most effective technique (it adds that extra, *contrast*) to acknowledge the exception or the opposition at the outset—and then knock it
down as soon as possible.

Sometimes an author opens with a statement of the opposing
view, intending to disprove it. In my article, "Do You Dare To
Be Honest in Marriage?" (*Today's Health*), the title is the
opening question, answered by:

> Now let the record be clear to start. Marriage should be based
> on truth. Any two people heading for the altar are also headed for
> trouble unless they've been honest about things that count. . . .
> (specifically cited)
> But beyond this firm foundation there is a wide area where
> it is both personally expedient and often downright wholesome,
> to touch up or trim down the truth.

Before you challenge this with arguments, *concede* certain
points. In a fine personal observation piece "Something's Happening Out There!" (*Family Circle*), newsman Charles Kuralt
sets out to disprove the common accusation that our country
has gone rotten: "We are so accustomed to hearing those things
about ourselves that we've come to believe them. Well, I don't
believe them any more." He then acknowledges:

> I know America has problems . . . I've heard the ignorant
> words of racial abuse . . . seen the cities' slums and migrant
> workers' shacks. . . . What saves me from despair is that, after
> reading about these aberrations I fold the paper and step into . . .
> the real country. [A country that he insists is still] as sturdy as a
> New England fishing boat and as lively as a Georgia fiddle tune.

Returning now to Pattern One:

Having taken care of the opposition, enlarge upon the first anecdote or introduce others to illustrate your point. You can, of course, do both. Meanwhile, continue to discuss and prove that point or theme. In other words, link these illustrations through your own comments. Then conclude with some definite suggestions.

In "Let Us Speak to One Another," Ardis Whitman accomplished this by asking, "What can we do about it?" then suggesting several ways to achieve significant communication between human beings: improving your own voice, learning to think and speak more clearly, learning to listen, learning truly to feel for others. She then summarizes and "ties a bow on the package" with this statement:

> No one can wholly understand another human being; no one can be wholly understood. But now and again, if we try, we can be brave enough to make ourselves known . . . At such moments, life is at its best for each of us and we have made a small contribution to a world whose people need, as they never needed before, the gift of speaking to each other in trust and understanding.

A study of published articles will reveal how consistently this particular pattern, with its list of final rules or suggestions, is followed.

Pattern Two is simply a variation of Pattern One.

Open with either one good anecdote or a discussion of your theme. Then, instead of putting the specific suggestions at the end, build the entire body of your article upon them. For anyone who has trouble with organization, this is an excellent device. Time and again, struggling with material that somehow would not fall smoothly into place, I have started over, using the 1. 2. 3. method, and had the article surge successfully forward. It is also a form the reader finds easy to follow.

To illustrate, let's analyze an article I wrote for *Family Circle,* entitled "Goodbye, Family—Hello, World!"

The anecdotal opening is as follows:

> Mrs. Jackson swept the last grains of rice from the rug, carried the final box of tissue paper to the attic, and sat down on the steps to face a shocking fact: Daughter Judy was married now; son David a junior in college. While Bill, just out of high school, was expecting his army call. "Why, I'm *through!*" thought Mrs. Jackson. "My husband has twenty years still with his company— I haven't *any* more years with mine. I'm about to retire!"

This is followed by five paragraphs contrasting the plight of today's modish matron who bids her family goodbye, with her sisters of the past who died younger or were reconciled to the fact that they were "getting on." How will Mrs. Jackson spend the second half of her life? the article asks. And how can each younger Mrs. Jackson prepare now for that inevitable time?

The article then presents six definite items of advice, each followed by two or three paragraphs of discussion and anecdote pertinent to that suggestion:

> 1. She can give her "retirement" thoughtful attention while her flock is still around.
>   Children are noisy creatures that sometimes drive us crazy. The best mother is occasionally guilty of thinking, "I'll be glad when they're gone. . . ."
> 2. She can begin developing inner resources.
>   The busiest mother should practice solitude. Get up half an hour earlier, if necessary, to start the day in peace. A neighbor of mine. . . .
> 3. She can guard against becoming too wrapped up in her family.
>   I know a woman whose horizons are limited by a line of diapers, whose entire conversation is the brilliance of (or injuries to) her offspring. Aside from being a crashing bore. . . .

My article then explores the vast field of public service and cites definite places where women are finding rich rewards in helping the rest of the world go 'round.

The conclusion then wraps the whole thing up by reverting right back to the opening:

There is no reason for any Mrs. Jackson to dread her time of retirement. No excuse for self-pity, for squandering the precious years that can mean so much in self-discovery and the thrill of the outgoing heart. Certainly not if she starts preparing now.

If she does, she won't be sitting on the bottom step for long. She'll realize with a sense of adventure: "Goodbye, Family— Hello, World!"

As I have said, you needn't be bound by these patterns. You may be sufficiently ingenious to create your own from time to time. But if you write very many creative articles, you'll find yourself following one of these patterns, often without even planning to, because they're so natural a method of persuasive expression. And if you do have a good idea and don't know quite how to present it, try Pattern One or Two. Like our hypothetical heroine, you won't sit staring into space (or at your typewriter) for long.

5

Tone, Focus, and Pace

There is a subtle but real relationship between tone and style. Actually, the tone of an article is in part created by the style in which it is written. But there is another very important aspect of tone which comes from the author's own emotions and point of view.

Two equally fine symphony orchestras composed of the same instruments may play the same composition, but the music will sound very different—first, because of their particular styles and second, because of their special tones.

The writer, as conductor, is using words with all the skill at his command. He may be a humorist who writes a clever piece, yet it fails because it sounds smug, unkind, contemptuous. Or the writer may be a woman describing how she coped with sorrow. Her story may be valid and essentially moving; she may have organized it well; the writing may be smooth. Yet again it may fall flat because it is depressing or smacks of self-pity, or contrarily be even too glib in its resolution. If so, the whole thing *sounds* wrong, she has simply hit upon the wrong *tone*.

Generally speaking, creative articles should be pleasantly conversational in tone. Advice articles definitely should be so, otherwise their tone will become bossy, preachy, didactic. Articles with the light touch, straight humor or otherwise, should never sound coy, self-conscious or cute. Their tone should be gay without being flippant. Articles of inspirational quality should sound gentle, even tender, but never sentimental or sticky sweet. Articles of controversy or protest should sound forceful and even angry in places, but never caustic, sarcastic, or too grim. Otherwise, they become diatribe, their storm and fury repelling the reader instead of interesting and arousing him. Articles of personal experience should neither smack of "poor me," nor swagger and boast. Another tone that sometimes slips into such articles is one of amazement: how exciting it all was, how frightened we were, how relieved at last. And it should be self-evident that any thoughtful article on any serious subject should never slip into coyness or flippancy or any other sins which jar the general tone.

There should be a prevailing mood or tone, deriving from four elements: the author's *style;* his *attitude* toward his material; the *point of view* from which the author writes the article; and the *basic premise* or point he is trying to make.

All or several of these elements are, surprisingly, lacking in many amateurs' attempts at creative articles. Unsure of their own viewpoints, confused in their attitudes, never quite able to pin down the actual premise, the authors of such articles write too much about too little, and achieve no satisfactory overall tone.

It will be helpful, I hope, to examine the factors which can produce the wrong tone.

Wrong subject

True, anything in the world can be written about humorously or gently or constructively if the treatment results in the appropriate tone. But some subjects are better avoided, unless you are careful—minority groups, for instance; classes of people, especially the service classes (truck and cab drivers, waitresses, hairdressers, maids, etc.); the handicapped and the under-privileged.

In the creative article, of course, we are not dealing with

classes or particular conditions of people per se. We are dealing
with human behavior, with emotions, with philosophy. But if
any one kind or class of people provides your major illustration, you must bring a special measure of understanding to the
task.

To illustrate: I have before me a student manuscript which
is supposed to be funny, and could be. The writing itself is
deft, the wisecracks witty. The subject, however, is borderline:
a wife's running battle with waitresses—a subject that could
be hilarious, if skillfully handled, or become downright embarrassing and unkind.

The opening is brisk:

> Tonight I look forward to having a good dinner after my wife's
> fight. If I've given the impression that my wife is a woman wrestler,
> I should explain. I'm referring to her fight with waitresses in any
> restaurant to which I take her. From the first moment she and a
> waitress lock eyes, there is a sensed hostility, as if they were but
> renewing old wars waged on distant battlefields of long ago. . . .
> It goes like this—

He orders a table for two, and assures the reader that his
wife is a very sweet person under any other circumstance. But
now the inevitable is about to begin. By the third paragraph,
I, along with the husband, was beginning to feel embarrassed.
By the fourth I was squirming before the wife's unreasoning
rudeness. By the fifth I wanted to smack her for being so nasty
to "Big Bertha," the outsized, slow-moving waitress. And when
the wife sent back her steak and she and her husband left,
laughing gaily at the waitress' consternation, I was filled with
sad dismay. No amount of clever writing can compensate
for cruelty. What might have been an amusing satire about a
wife's peccadillo, simply makes fun of a less fortunate human
being. The tone of the entire piece is ridicule.

Earlier I gave as a bad example the slapstick treatment of a
funeral. Any article dealing with any aspect of death must be
done very perceptively and sensitively indeed to strike a tone

that will not offend. Or, almost as bad, get overemotional. After class one day a beautiful woman came to me with tears in her eyes, beseeching me to criticize an account she had written of her little girl's fatal accident. I accepted it with apprehension, praying that it would be well done—since I shrank from adding further to her hurt. But tragedy is very hard to discuss, especially if its wounds are recent. The grief-stricken tone plunged the piece into melodrama. Such outpourings are not articles; they are soul purges that are better left in the desk drawer. I told her to put her article away and not even try to write of this experience until she could bring some detachment to it. I advised her to write on other subjects.

In the skilled hands of a John Gunther (*Death Be Not Proud*), or an Owenita Sanderlin (*Johnny,* the story of the loss of an equally promising son), such tragedies can be moving and inspiring to others. But the unseasoned writer would do well to choose other topics.

As for physical afflictions—your long bout with illness, your operation—there *is* a tremendous reader interest in health and the human body, in how to overcome the enemies that beset it. But so many people deluge editors with badly written blow-by-blow descriptions, written in the tone of "let me tell about my operation!" that your treatment in the article must be exceptional to merit consideration.

Well, what about sex? Now *there's* a sure-fire subject. Or is it? Don't be seduced by all that sex you see on magazine covers. Writing about sex and achieving just the right tone is a very difficult thing to do. Unless your attitudes are very sound and your writing very good, leave sex to the sexperts.

Wrong attitude

A perfectly safe subject such as home, children, friends, can be ruined by an attitude of condescension, superiority, and egotism on the author's part. If you bring any of these attitudes to your material, no matter how good your writing, fine your

organization, or cogent your arguments, that attitude will per-
meate and subtly poison the entire piece.

I have been guilty of this on several occasions. Years ago,
provoked by a certain person who continually free-loaded, bor-
rowed without returning, and was a born brain-picker, I wrote
an article deploring such traits. In order not to offend the original model, I parceled these traits out among a number of hypothetical, obnoxious characters. The whole thing stood up
technically, but my attitude of utter annoyance and chagrin
over something I was too weak to correct, wrecked the tone.
It was not pleasant reading.

I have had to revise articles about raising children. "Forgive
me but you sound a little superior," one editor wrote. A rereading proved her right—I certainly did. I had *felt* superior in
relating the wise and wonderful methods we were using in
raising our children, as contrasted to the mistakes some other
parents were making. (Such egotism is less of a hazard as you
grow older! In fact, you're less prone to preach to parents
about anything.)

Preaching is another tone that results from self-righteousness.
"We buy articles, not sermons!" an editor once scribbled across
the face of one of my early efforts. I was angry and hurt—but
she was actually doing me a favor. I remembered to keep out
of the pulpit, to speak with humility as well as conviction in the
articles I wrote thereafter.

Self-pity is an attitude to guard against. Feeling lonely and
unloved, or overwhelmed by the sheer unfairness of it all, we
are sometimes inspired to sit down and write away our miseries.
This can be excellent therapy, but it does not make for salable
articles. Other people are so busy feeling sorry for themselves
they don't want to be bothered feeling sorry for you. If they
are to share your wretchedness in any constructive way, it will
be because your *attitude* states clearly, "Look, I know I'm not
the only one. I tackled this problem or this situation in this way
and came out better for it. So can you." But again your attitude
cannot be, "how brave I am." I once worked on a manuscript

for a woman who devoted years to finding help for a mentally disturbed child. Her experiences were dramatic, and she showed real courage and gallantry. But repeatedly I had to warn, "Don't sound so sorry for yourself." Or, "Don't pose. You're just too self-consciously brave here."

Not all negative attitudes are wrong. Indignation, impatience, outrage—all can be effective occasionally. They can even be converted into something amusing. For a while I tapped a lucrative vein that came straight out of an attitude of distress: "Guests I Detest," "Hostesses I Abhor," "How to Lose Your Mailman," "How to Punish the Plumber." But the attitude of female fury and flurry succeeded because it was not meant to belittle or hurt anyone; it was simply good-humored satire of everybody's foibles, and the *tone* of good humor kept it fun.

You will find examples of friendly but funny annoyances in almost every magazine that uses humor, and from the syndicated columnists to items in your local paper. Jean Anne Seagren, who writes for my home town Storm Lake, Iowa, *Pilot Tribune,* came up with this honey, "Things the Bridal Guides Don't Tell You."

SIX MONTHS BEFORE THE WEDDING . . . The guide says to decide on type, place, date and hour. It doesn't give a hint as to how, six months in advance, you can avoid scheduling the ceremony on the same day as the big football game . . . The guide tells you to set the overall budget with your parents. It doesn't suggest how to revive your father when he discovers how your plans will wreck his bank account. . . .

THREE MONTHS BEFORE THE WEDDING . . . The guide tells you to complete the guest list, but not how to keep it within reason without hurting people's feelings . . . You are reminded to order the invitations, but not how many extra envelopes you'll need for those you'll ruin. . . . Some helpful suggestions that are not even mentioned are—paint the living room; go on a diet; and start hinting to your groom-to-be that he shave off his beard.

If the writer is seriously concerned about something, however, his attitude should show it. "Get mad!" an editor once urged in asking me to revise a piece of mild protest. "Let 'em

have it." In this instance, my attitude was wrong primarily because I wasn't sufficiently incensed. And if I weren't personally
aroused, why should anyone else be?

Currently, I *am* mad at what seems to me the invasion of *my*
privacy by having the sex lives of total strangers thrust upon
me. Fed up, I queried *Reader's Digest* about "A Plea For Some
Old-Fashioned Privacy," which they assigned and bought. It
was also published in *The PTA Magazine,* where it was spotted
by a child psychologist and used in a court case concerning the
damage such material can do to children.

Write while the adrenaline is still surging. Furious at the
flagrant anti-Americanism of some of Yevtushenko's poems
read at his New York concert, I flew home from Madison Square
Garden to compose "An Open Letter to Yevtushenko," where I
challenged him to accord me the same freedom and facilities to
attack Communism in the Kremlin. The letters that poured in
from that one—mostly from refugees and Soviet victims—
again proved that these articles of passionate protest or exhor-
tation can have far-reaching effects.

No point of view

If you have no clear point of view, you can make no point.
Thus you will have produced an article that really has nothing
to say, and so cannot achieve the quality of total tone.

As I said initially, the author of creative articles generally
approaches problems with both logic and emotion. He cannot
hurl himself sobbing into the article (as in the example of the
bereaved mother) or he will lose all sense of logic, and with it
his *point of view.* Neither can he remain detached from his
material. Logic alone will then prevail, minus any emotional
involvement; he will have lost that passion, that conviction,
that again results in *point of view.*

This may seem like a complicated way of stating a very
simple point. But think about it a minute, and I believe you'll
agree. You must have not only one definite, desirable *attitude*

toward your subject; you must also be very clear about where you stand on it. To determine this, first ask: What is this article all about? When you have established that, you can proceed to turn out a work which says something, holds together, and achieves the right tone. When you do not—when you bring in too many subjects, cover too much material, explore too many emotions, display diverse attitudes—the article winds up a hodge-podge, lacking any single tone, or worse, so out of focus that the theme cannot come through.

Focus

Focus is very important to an article. This means simply that the picture it portrays is clear instead of fuzzy and diffuse. A photographer has to train his camera on a subject and adjust his lens so that the result will be sharp and unmistakable—in short, in focus. The writer must do exactly the same thing. Newspaper writers call the central point of any story, their "angle." I have referred to it earlier as your "angle of interpretation." When we speak of focus, we mean simply concentrating upon that angle.

The writer must decide what his subject actually is. And then bring to it only material that will contribute to the final, unmistakable effect. Every sentence must somehow achieve this purpose or it is extraneous and must be ruthlessly cut out.

"But this will make my article read like an outline!" protested one student who had written 3,000 words that so fogged and clouded what I presumed was her original image that I proposed cutting the article in half. She herself was not sure just what her article was trying to say. By discarding half of what she had written and sternly focusing all the rest on one specific phase, or angle, of her discussion, there was a chance of saving it. Actually, however, the entire 3,000 words might have had a legitimate excuse for being there had they been so arranged and directed that they *emphasized her point,* rather than diverting the reader from it.

Before you can learn to focus, you must decide: What is this article all about? What is its basic message or theme?

Here are some examples:

The manuscript just referred to began promisingly: An opening anecdote in which the author described her first reactions to the loss of her husband. The sense of loneliness, of being at loose ends, of trying to find some reason for going on. . . . Yes, yes, *do* go on—but not much farther! I began to react. Get to the point. How did you solve this important and common problem? What do you propose?

Well, first she visited her sister in Boston, and then she remembered her childhood days in Texas, and next she seemed to be on a boat to Europe with a description of fellow passengers. Then she was in Athens, where the taxi drivers must be watched, and the food is good at a little place just off Syntagma Square, and from her windows she could look down on the old Royal Palace, now the home of the Greek Parliament, and after a few days exploring the ruins there—

What emerged from many pages was neither advice nor philosophy, neither personal adventure nor travelogue. The article was long, wordy and totally disorganized, mainly because it had no focus. It had no overriding purpose or ultimate message. It said a lot about too many things, and in the end had nothing to say.

Or take a manuscript by another student, in a lighter vein: The title was so delightful she may still be able to use it, so I won't give it away here. A rough and very inferior paraphrase: "You Kids Lay Off My Piano." Written by a piano teacher, it started out describing the havoc pupils can wreak on the instructor's instrument. They bang it, they kick it, they often scratch it with pencils, rulers or their fingernails. So far, so good. The article could have been amusing, exploring this hazard further. Or it could have led into a light but firm discussion as to how to train the little demons to avert the damage— to both instrument and teacher's temper.

There were two excellent possibilities, in fact, either one of which could have been briskly and engagingly followed. But, no. We were presently learning about music conservatories, their cost, merits and locations. And about the author's childhood, and how hard she had to practice. Then came something about her romance with a tall, handsome harpist, and how he didn't want her to give piano lessons; and about her mother's old piano, which had a much better sounding board than those you get, especially in spinets, today.

As the words piled up, I began to count, in a kind of fascination, the angles on which she might have focused to draw a good article out of this loosely thrown together batch of material, and bemoaned the fact that if she had only decided *which one* she was going to emphasize, she could have made the other incidents, disparate though they were, related to that central objective. Each little tale or argument could have been trimmed and shaped to fit neatly into the framework of her composition.

Or, again, she might have focused on the career of a piano teacher: Her own childhood experiences leading up to this hour; the opposition of her husband; her ultimate trials and triumphs. It might have focused on pianos themselves, her mother's sturdy instrument vs. those today; how to choose one that can stand up under the onslaught of bratty kids.

By deciding on her angle and bringing it into focus, she might have used every incident to lighten, shade, enhance, or clarify her central subject. It would have had some reason for being there. Instead, we had a batch of mildly interesting ideas going in their different directions, resulting only in confusion and fuzziness.

Cures

Here are a few suggestions to cure this confusion and restore focus:

1. Cut everything that does not bear directly upon your

point. In the case of the bereaved widow, this would eliminate lengthy descriptions of problems with customs agents and people encountered on the ship, for instance.

2. If you feel that some section has an obscure bearing on your point and you want to keep it, *refocus,* reshape, and reslant that particular material so that it does relate directly to your central theme.

To illustrate, even a hassle with customs agents *could* be made to bear upon the problems of a widow traveling alone for the first time. ("The whole world may seem to be against her at first—this stranger pawing through the luggage. . . .") Or encounters on shipboard could be turned into anecdotes that helped to prove or disprove something. (People's solicitude, or their indifference. Discovering others with a similar problem, how sharing helps, advice received, etc.)

But unless something serves to sharpen up the angle, or make your theme more significant, it has no business there.

3. Put a figure of speech to work.

In a fine, thoughtful, intelligently funny book, *Sex is Dead,* the Episcopal chaplain Earl H. Brill uses an old but strong analogy, a dam:

> Freud found a culture which had *dammed up* the human sex drive behind a *great wall* of repression. He made *a few cracks in the wall* and was astonished at the force of the *torrent* that poured out. He concluded that here, indeed, was the great *reservoir* of energy which drives human personality.*

He continues to use the analogy to draw together, sharpen, keep in focus several elements that might have gone wandering off and become ineffectual: Society since Freud's time, changing attitudes since Puritan and Victorian days, how vast areas of joy and "sexuality" have not even been tapped yet, and today's opportunists who are exploiting sex drives for commercial ends. He keeps all this firmly cohesive and clear by leaning

* From SEX IS DEAD *and Other Post Mortems,* by Earl Brill. © 1967, by The Seabury Press, New York.

constantly on that dam: "We might conclude that *flood con-ditions* are only temporary . . ." "Opportunists who have been making their living off the flood waters have *turned to the pumps* to keep the water at a high level through artificial means—" (Italics mine.)

Though Chaplain Brill has flooded a lot of territory, the reader isn't futilely trying to swim to some undefined shore. He knows exactly where the author is taking him.

Pace

If you keep your point clearly in focus, you are far more likely to achieve that precious sense of timing known as pace. Pace is absolutely essential to any form of writing.

Pace is movement. Pace is a sense of forward motion that is always smooth and rhythmic as it leads—or carries—the reader swiftly toward the goal.

An appropriate analogy is horse racing. As youngsters we used to watch the harness races at the county fair. When the gun went off, the horses sprang forward, pulling their little carts behind them. Then, very often as the crowd cheered a favorite rounding a far corner, a mass groan would go up: "Oh, he broke, he's lost his pace!" That is the original term, and no doubt where writers actually got it. And how accurate it is! Just as a horse who loses his stride in any way cannot hope to finish a winner, neither can an article or short story. It too must surge swiftly ahead, pounding out its smooth, inevitable rhythms. It cannot jump fences to explore neighboring pas-tures, go back to the gate to start over, pause to nibble grass, shy at bright objects, or balk. It must run confidently forward. Then stop.

Pace is partly a matter of style, a delicate balancing of the phrases that carry the writer's thoughts. As you progress as a writer, you begin to develop a sixth sense of timing or pace. Even when you use the flashback technique (cutting back in sequence of events to supply information), that sense of forward motion is still there. Since the seeming interruption, the flashback, occurs for the purpose of leading right back to the present and beyond it, the subtle, steady beat of pace continues to be felt.

The more you write, the more skilled you will become at controlling that vital element, pace.

The tone. The focus. The pace. Observe them as you read. Make them a part of your inner awareness. Elusive as they are, they are important; mark them in the margins of your consciousness.

6

Making a Good Article Better

There are other elements that you should keep in mind to help you sell your article: contrast and comparison, color, timeliness, specifics, memory devices. All are valuable.

Contrast and comparison

Contrast and comparison keep your tone from becoming a *monotone*. They flow subtly but effectively through the best creative articles, in the following ways:

a) acknowledging the opposition viewpoint
b) contrasting past with present
c) comparing the desirable with the undesirable
d) comparing types of people, customs, attitudes, things

In short, by putting any two opposites in juxtaposition; or by showing variations of the same thing. We do this continually in the things we think and say (by comparing ourselves with others, for instance). Sometimes comparison makes us miserable; sometimes it spurs us on. Nonetheless, it is inescapable. In writing the creative article—which is actually a reflection of life—comparison is so natural a method that I marvel that so many would-be writers fail to utilize it.

Watch for it as you read published articles. Slight as it may seem, it is there for a purpose. Comparison and contrast enhance the point and enliven the tone.

In his fine article, "How Wonderful You Are," which appeared first in *Woman's Day,* then in *Reader's Digest,* author Arthur Gordon opens with a long and lovely anecdote which demonstrates how much more freely people expressed emotions in the past. "The people in those generations cared about one another, enormously and intimately. And they said so." To illustrate, he quotes from some old letters wherein love and admiration were generously expressed. He then compares this with circumstances today.

> Such loyalty and affection were implicit, I knew, in my own family relationships, but they were seldom expressed, and certainly not in a forthright way. Somewhere along the line, my generation had put a checkrein on the release of such emotions. To give utterance to them became corny, somehow faintly foolish. It was out of fashion; it just wasn't done. I don't pretend to know what brought this change about, but I do know this: it seriously interferes with one of the deepest of all human needs—the desire for acceptance and approval by other people.

This point is then proved by citing the advantages that accrue to any individual who is aware of being appreciated. And here again contrast is used by stating:

> The converse is also true. . . . If you think people are critical or even indifferent, your self-esteem shrinks, and with it your capacity for living.

Then, really sharpening up this effective tool, he wields it even more tellingly by contrasting two groups of writers at the University of Wisconsin. The men's group called The Stranglers were merciless in their criticism of each other's manuscripts. The women's, like their milder name, The Wranglers, were more gentle,

> hunting for kind things to say. All efforts, however feeble, were encouraged. The payoff came about twenty years later:—Of all the bright young talents in The Stranglers, not one had made a literary reputation of any kind. Out of The Wranglers had come half a dozen successful writers, some of national prominence, led by Marjorie Kinnan Rawlings.

Comparison and contrast give the reader perspective. They weave the various arguments and facets of the piece together to add to its cohesiveness. They enable the author to enhance his point and enliven his tone. Watch for them in published articles; mark them with a CC or some other symbol. Then study your own manuscripts to see where you can employ comparison and contrast.

Color

Black-and-white television was wonderful. But ask anyone who has a color set if he's been watching more television since getting it. It's difficult to imagine being satisfied with the old. The world lies before us in living color, and the eye is equipped to enjoy it. So too is the mental eye. And while countless very fine articles are published in simple black and white, a touch of color adds to the pleasure.

Shortly after John P. Marquand died, the *Saturday Review* published a two-part tribute to him. The first part, "The Man" by John Mason Brown, is so truly creative an article, and so rich in color, that I read it to my classes. The following excerpt seems to me a perfect example of the use of color:

> His were the bluest eyes I have ever seen and they became bluer when he was amused . . . His eyes seemed the bluer, and his carefully combed white hair the whiter and his dark eyebrows the blacker because of the accentuating pinkness of his skin, which in explosive moments could become poppy-red. . . .

It is as if, among all the other beautifully phrased characteristics, we were suddenly seeing the man himself "in living color" before us, or on a screen.

In the personal essay or the nostalgic article, opportunities for color abound. Don't just wrap a blanket around the baby— color it yellow. When the frost is on the pumpkin, make it an orange pumpkin, and the youngster who's carrying it up the hill clad in blue jeans or a bright red mackinaw. Be careful, of course, not to overdo this; color isn't something to be recklessly splashed around. But if you've written a good piece in black and white and want to brighten it up, go over it with a careful paintbrush. You'll be surprised at how many places there are where a touch of color, like a touch of humor, will make it glow.

Characterization

The creative article depends upon anecdotes, which involve people. You don't *have* to characterize as you do in writing fiction; there is simply no space to go deeply into motivation or to add much description. But your work has an extra dimension and appeal if you make your people genuine individuals when you can. Just as in fiction, people do characterize themselves by what they say, and how they act or look. The trick of the article writer is to compress this into a few words.

Let's look again at Hildegarde Dolson's lively, "I Love a Nice Liar":

> Perhaps I'm particularly susceptible to a good snow job because, in my youth, I had a daily dose of candor from a schoolmate named Maribelle. You know how they say of somebody, "She's so honest it hurts?" That was Maribelle. I still bear the scars.
>
> I remember the afternoon at Conneaut Lake, where my mother had taken a group of us swimming. When I appeared in my bathing suit, Maribelle surveyed me thoughtfully with unblinking blue eyes. "Goodness, you're bony!" she said in a voice as clear as rock crystal. "Your chest looks like the slats in a venetian blind."

A less able writer might have said: "Perhaps I'm susceptible to flattery because as a girl I had a very frank schoolmate who often hurt my feelings. I remember one afternoon when my mother had taken us swimming. When I appeared in my bathing suit the girl remarked on how skinny I was." This would be adequate to cover the situation, but flat as her chest, compared to the portrait of a catty girl named Maribelle, who "surveyed me thoughtfully with unblinking blue eyes" (color) and "in a voice as clear as rock crystal," said "Goodness, you're bony! Your chest looks like the slats in a venetian blind."

In a more serious article, "The Lesson of the Gracious Heart," in *Together*, Elizabeth Byrd refers to her bus seat companion on the way to Inverness, Scotland, as "a big raw-boned farm woman," who remarks, "It's rooky weather in the highlands." James Stewart Gordon's "Relax and Get Fit!" (*Today's Health*) is not a creative article in the narrow sense, but how creative is this character description: "Gosta Olander, a wispy snowflake of a man with an electric smile and muscles like the cables of a ski lift—"

Opportunities for characterization are plentiful in humorous articles or the personal sketch. In "Drip and Hang up to Dry" (*Harper's Bazaar* and *Reader's Digest*), Malcolm Bradbury introduces himself:

> I once came over from England, a tall, feckless youth with long hair and thick tweedy suits, to teach a course in English composition to uninterested freshmen in a state university in the Middle West.

This bit of description isn't really necessary to his ensuing adventures with drip-dry clothes, but it makes him a vital human being, hence his experiences more fun to follow.

The ability to draw vivid characters *is* important to articles of reminiscence, and in some instances to articles of personal experience. It's less important elsewhere, but since the creative article is akin to fiction, you'll find it more fun to write if you characterize where you logically can. It gives your work that extra quality that lifts it out of the ordinary.

Timeliness

The creative article writer deals with the verities of life, which are timeless. He does not have to keep "one step ahead of the news" in the way journalists do, or deal with current events in the same manner as fact writers. But he *must* keep up to date. His approach to whatever topic he chooses must be thoroughly modern.

For instance, it would be pretty silly to deal with the perennial problem of money in terms of the Depression (unless you are carefully translating experiences from that period in the thirties into lessons applicable today), or to discuss the dilemma of wives with husbands off serving in Korea or previous wars. You would have to write with reference to whatever current mess we happen to be in.

Concerning style, if some word, phrase, or bit of slang currently in vogue will emphasize or perk up your point, by all means use it. You're not writing for posterity here. But don't *back*date your article by Victorian language (" 'twas", "the lad informed me" etc.), or slang already grown quaint with age, or merely sophomoric phrases like "wow-de-dow!" "oh, yeah?" or "boy, oh boy!"

An otherwise good article can be ruined by has-been comparisons. The article about the wife who fought with waitresses, was dated in this manner: The waitress bellowed "in a voice like Lauritz Melchoir," and "Primo Carnera would have been intimidated." The writer mentioned Dempsey, Tunney, Joan Crawford, Zachary Scott. All figures who are, unfortunately, either dead or no longer as prominent as they once were.

An article should sound timely in all its aspects. Yet for some curious reason many writers, even young ones, reach *back* for their comparisons and examples. This is great if you are writing nostalgia—then your illustrations ought to come straight from Grandma's attic. You are intentionally establishing datedness. But in all other instances the writer should sound as modern as possible. People who make headlines change, and so do skirt lengths, dances, and popular songs. Remember this when revising.

A good article can be made brighter and better by references to contemporary figures, styles, fads, controversies, or anything else on the immediate scene. They give the reader a little start of recognition. He feels you're with it, and so is he. But be sure your analogies, quips and references *are* modern.

Specifics

The creative article is based upon the intangible—ideas. To make those ideas graphic, we pin them down with specifics. We give specific illustrations. We often give the characters in those illustrations specific characteristics and callings. Then, as we attempt to demonstrate the basic premise, we go a step further, adding color and interest through more specifics.

Take the following general statement, for example:

> What people discard these days is as good as lots of things we used to save. Everywhere I go I see stuff that is still fairly new and a shame to throw away, especially in view of the emphasis on ecology. My mother would have been a specialist at recycling things. She was so economical she put everything to several uses—medicines, toilet articles, kitchen equipment, and she knew how to save food.

Now compare this with the paragraph as it appeared in print. Even condensed from the original in *New York Sunday News,* Sam Levenson's details paint word pictures that add vitality.

> What poor as well as rich families leave on the sidewalks these days for the Sanitation Department to cart away looks to me like the stuff people used to load on moving vans, not on dump trucks. I see lamps, umbrellas, TV sets, playpens, baby carriages, bicycles. . . . My mother did not know words like ecology, but sometimes out of necessity, but as often out of sheer ingenuity, Mama invented uses for things . . .
> A little castor oil would make anything go faster—clocks, fans, drills, or kids; a brand-new toilet plunger stuck on the bathroom wall near the sink made a great towel rack; a few drops of camphor oil in a gas-steam iron and you could press a shirt and cure a cough at the same time . . .

The skilled humorist doesn't just tell us that Mama was thrifty and ingenious; his entire piece gives us lively, loving, *specifics* whereby she saved the family money; and he draws a charming character sketch at the same time.

Here is another example, taken from an article in which I challenged the popular notion that you're a bad parent if you don't participate in all your children's activities:

General

I was finally cured of this idea. When people think they can always count on you for all the work, some may be impressed, but mostly you just get blamed.

Specific

The penalties of being little old Mr. or Mrs. Dependable, who can always be counted on to *run the school bazaar, chaperone the dances,* and *haul the uniformed troops and tribes* to their supposedly beneficial destinations, can far outweigh the values. . . . The absolute height of some people's reactions is to murmur, "My goodness, I just don't see how she does it," as they *reach for another nibble of salted nuts* and *reflect on their bridge hands.*

Often you are blamed for everything that goes wrong. "See here, my child was *20 minutes late getting home from Bluebirds* and we always *eat at six.*" Or, "*Jimmy got sick* after the *church picnic.* It does seem to me that those in charge could have *made sure the potato salad was fresh.*"

I have italicized the specifics to make them stand out. The published version is not only more effective because more fervent, it spares us banal generalities.

Here are two treatments of my nostalgic article, "Whatever Happened to Run, Sheep, Run?" from *Today's Health:*

General

I often wonder whatever happened to the games we used to play after supper as children? And where are the youngsters who used to enjoy them so much? I suppose they're all grown up now, like me, and their children tease to go out and play, just as we did.

Specific

Whatever happened, I sometimes wonder, to Hide-and-Seek? And Pump, Pump, Pull-Away and Old Gray Wolf? And where are the children who used to trample gardens, clamber over fences, and shatter the quiet darkness with their cries of "Run, Sheep, Run!" They're now suburban housewives, like me, I suppose, or busy commuting dads. And their offspring are just as eager as we were to play out-of-doors after supper. You can hear them now at their games of kick-ball in the street. And they're mad about something called Muck-a-Ny. But Hide-and-Seek? Old Gray Wolf? And *what* was Run, Sheep, Run?

Generalized writing may be adequate; and if you are producing essays for profoundly thoughtful literary journals (and your style is otherwise impressive) it may even be preferred. But if you are aiming for popular magazines, be definite. Make choices. Don't simply plant flowers—put them in window pots and decide on geraniums (or petunias); don't have a wife merely cook a husband's favorite dish—decide (even as she must) which dish it shall be. Pot roast? Shrimp Creole or cheese fondue? It doesn't matter; what does matter is that *you* serve the reader a definite image.

It is these details, small but colorful and concrete, that give the creative article a plus factor, another extra to help it sell.

A memory device

My son, home from Coast Guard boot camp, was enthusiastic about a certain lecturer he had heard. "He was marvelous, he made us realize so many things I hadn't thought of, and that I'll never forget. He put it something like this—the Four M's. Manhood. Money. Matrimony. And wound up with the Message—is your life going to be a message or just a mess?"

I gave a little start. Here was a boy who usually pulled down his mental shades at lectures, who didn't even care about books. Yet he had not only listened, he was quoting words he declared would influence him all his life. This speaker had recognized how amorphous are abstract ideas, unless one can both activate them through graphic illustrations and then etch them into the mind of the audience. He had succeeded with these restless boys because of an ancient, simple memory device!

I had already read and written hundreds of idea articles, but not until that moment did it dawn on me that this is what good writers and speakers do continually. By accident or deliberate design, we seek to make our thoughts easier to follow and, hopefully, harder to forget. And very often this is accomplished by some small but effective device.

Methods

Going through my own published articles, and a great many others, I discovered that methods vary and most of them are not really unique. But the fact that they are used so frequently proves their worth.

Here's what I mean:

1. Enumerating

A list of rulés or suggestions numbered 1, 2, 3. This is a good way to organize and write an article; or a good way to summarize. It also qualifies as a memory device.

2. Alphabetizing, or alliteration

Margaret Blair Johnstone did this to perfection in one of the best examples of the creative article you'll ever read (good articles have everything), "What Makes Courage?" an original for *Reader's Digest*. What makes courage? she asks after anecdote and discussion. "For this we need first, *perspective*. . . . A second ingredient of courage is *perseverance*. . . . The third ingredient we need for courage is *principle*."

Notice that she goes even beyond the three P's, to make her first syllables match as well—*per* and *pr*.

3. The acrostic (making the first letter of the first word of key paragraphs spell out your point).

I used this device in one of my early pieces, "Seven Ways to Spell Husband", which sold, as I recall, to *Today's Woman* (Helpfulness, Understanding, Strength, etc.) I think I matched it up with "Four Ways to Spell Wife." This is very gimmicky indeed. I don't recommend it except for beginners who are trying their wings. This method shows, however, how a little trick helps you organize material and make it clear.

4. The symbol

We find the symbol used constantly in novels, plays and stories. An object, however insignificant in itself, *means* something. A teakettle, a jar of roses, a pair of yellow shoes may stand for something very important to the character and testify to some truth. Since the creative article is akin to fiction, how logical then that the symbol is often used. Particularly in the inspirational essay, personal experience, or article of advice.

Your symbol may crystallize your dominant theme, as in John Kord Lagemann's "Bring to It the Rainbow" (*Christian Herald, Reader's Digest*) mentioned earlier. After several examples of people who put extra efforts into their undertakings (splitting wood, shining shoes), he quotes Pablo Casals as telling a pupil, "Bring to it the rainbow," and explains, "The rainbow is the glow that crowns an all-out effort to do any kind of job."

I use symbols continually in writing my columns, *Love and Laughter*: A daughter's first sheer hose (first step into maturity, dating, a mother's sense of joy and loss); leading children across a busy street (if only you could lead them as safely through the dangers of life ahead); the real meaning of the doormat saying WELCOME on your step. And I have used symbols in numerous magazine sketches: "Dad, I Need Some Money" (*McCall's*) used a man's wallet as a symbol to represent the faithfulness with which fathers meet their family's needs. "The Family Table" (*American Home*) symbolized the unity and solidarity of "living people drawn together" and since this is an antique table, the life of families before.

Used in this manner, your symbol is not only a memory device, but it also sparks and fires the original idea. Begin to think in terms of symbols, and you will find a rich new source of ideas.

Again, the symbol may be something which crops up almost by accident at the beginning or the end of the article. This happened in the personal experience article about our son's catching and stuffing a huge marlin. The fish became his first major trophy. A trophy is important to a boy. But to be significant, a trophy has to be won or earned. While the article dealt with the humorous complications of two amateurs coping with an eight-foot fish, the message emerged and was pinned down by that symbol of the trophy, to conclude: "The real trophies aren't the ones you pay for with money."

5. Question and answer. Dialogue.

Dr. David Reuben proved how effective this form can be in his book *Everything You Always Wanted to Know About Sex But Were Afraid to Ask*. Each point is presented in one simple question. The author then answers, using illustrations. The whole thing reads like a taped interview. More and more fact writers are actually using tape recorders for interviews, which they skillfully edit before publication.

The question-answer or dialogue framework works equally well for the creative article. The difference is that your article can be based on any conversation, real or imagined, between two people, which clearly establishes the arguments you wish to make. It saves the writer a lot of straight exposition, and its brisk, natural conversational form makes it highly readable. A good example is "A Generation Gap?" by Arba and Nora Herr, in *The Christian Home*. Subtitled "The recollection of a mother-daughter conversation regarding values and life styles," it goes like this:

MRS. PARENT: . . . I have decided some things are just not worth raising the blood pressure for. But you had better believe this decision did not come easily! I would include style and fashion, long hair or short, sideburns, mustache or beard under this heading.

BETH: So clothes make the person? . . . My reasons for what I wear are important only to me and my self-concept. I wear "worn out, shapeless jeans" not as a badge of conformity to the youth culture but because they are 1. comfortable 2. cheap 3. practical.

MRS. P.: Maybe clothes aren't that important, but there are "growing pains" that could become a generation gap . . .

6. A letter, an ad, a TV commercial, or anything else you

can conjure up to package and make more tangible your basic idea

I began "What Became of the Girl You Married?" (*Better Homes and Gardens, Reader's Digest*) like this: *"Lost: One gay, sweet bride. Girl who thinks I'm wonderful, and tells me so. Chief characteristic: Appreciation! Ample reward offered by one discouraged guy."* Continuing, "Countless men could have composed that ad." Then, after citing the many areas in which women unwittingly fail our husbands, and emphasizing how important it is to show our appreciation, conclude the article: "The woman who can rediscover those virtues won't have to worry about romance. She'll have her share of it and something even better—a guy who'll be saying, in his heart: *"Found, the girl I married."*

A memory device is simply an extra. It is not necessary to the creative article. But once you become aware of its possibilities, you will use it more often. It can be very helpful to you as well as the reader. It helps to stitch together the scattered elements of your article and make them cohesive. And sometimes it will provide you with a lively and logical opening, to which you can tie a logical and impressive ending.

You will not find all the extras discussed here present in all the published articles you read. Yet experience has taught me that articles which are most interesting to write and easiest to sell are those which have an ingredient of originality and explicitness, an extra shine, a quality of truly caring on the part of the author. Those which "bring to it the rainbow."

7

Two Extras: Good Titles and Quotes

You have a sympathetic awareness of people. Your ideas are sound, fresh, and plentiful. You write well. You know, through instinct, observation, or practice, how to put articles together. In other words, you're like a cook who can prepare a balanced and nourishing meal. But now you want to make the setting more attractive, to add a few gourmet touches. I'm talking about those extras which make a good article better and help it sell. Let's take a close look at two of them—titles and quotes —and see how their flavor subtly enhances and livens up the whole.

Titles

Some writers say not to worry about titles, that the editor will probably change yours anyway. And it's true that some editors like to change titles—not always for the better. But a catchy title is important. It is the first thing an editor sees. If the title catches his attention, he proceeds, whereas a dull title puts you at a disadvantage to start.

How to produce intriguing titles? Sometimes we have to track them down; again one may simply appear from the subconscious and produce the spark for the article itself. The truly creative writer does a lot of thinking; his concepts of life are often encapsuled into simple, telling phrases. If he is attuned to listening for these phrases, he finds his title troubles at a minimum, and also his problem of getting ideas and *focusing on one aspect* to find the angle of interpretation.

For instance, when my husband was a graduate student, a group of us had wonderful parties playing cards and serving the cheapest possible foods in amusing ways. Since nobody could afford baby-sitters, the youngsters were brought along and bedded down. I did not consciously decide: "I shall write an article about being poor but happy." But one day, there popped into my mind the phrase: *Fun without funds*. And off I flew to knock out a little piece about the silly, refreshing things people can do without spending a lot of money. I recalled the days when Mother's ingenuity made our Christmas celebration seem abundant, even when Dad was out of a job. I made the point that such experiences are enriching.

Although this discussion is about titles, let me note here that the fact writer would have taken pictures of our little group, recorded interviews, perhaps produced statistics. But for a creative article, it was the philosophy that concerned me, and I could wander as far as imagination took me, *as long as I stuck to my major premise*.

Again, for no conceivable reason, there flashed into my consciousness one day the words: *Five ways to finish an affair*. At that time, being as naïve as Rebecca of Sunnybrook Farm, I didn't even know what an affair really was! Nonetheless, I wrote an earnest but lively article inventing advice for the woman who wants to discourage the attentions of a man. I sold it to a large magazine, and to my complete amazement (and the alarm of my husband) I was deluged with letters from women living far more colorful lives than mine.

But not all titles come unsought, of course. Nor does the basic idea always link itself with the perfect title. I often start off with a working title (anything that reasonably resembles what is to be discussed) or no title at all—then find the right title springing from the article as it is written. When this fails,

I walk away from the piece and let my subconscious wrestle with it for a while. Or I take another sheet of paper and write, as fast as I can, as many titles as I can. By using free association and a lot of alliteration, I find quite often that an excellent title will come.

If none of this works, and I'm still not satisfied, I sift out what seems to be the best choice.

Here are some examples of the various *kinds* of titles you can use. If you will fix them in mind and review them when you are having title trouble, you can't go too far astray. These types can also serve to stimulate your own article ideas:

1. *Alliterative titles*

Alliteration is the repetition of the initial sound in successive words. If not overdone, it makes your title sing: The following are some I've used: "Passport to Popularity," "The Whys of Working Wives," "Are You Teacher's Problem Parent?," "That Chronic Other Couple," "Don't Hang Onto Heartbreak," "What Makes Your Wife a Worrier?," "Men, Money and Marriage," "Hail to the Head of the House."

2. *How-to titles*

Everybody wants to know *how to* get more out of life, which is what the creative article is really all about. This includes learning how to do anything that concerns him better, whether it's *How to Win Friends and Influence People,* the famous book by Dale Carnegie, or *How to Get Ahead in Business without Really Trying,* the spoof by Shepherd Mead. Those two little words, "how to," are like a magic key. If you can legitimately tuck them into your title, you're ahead. (Warning—do not cheat; never use them unless the article does provide some specific aids or answers.)

Here's how to use them (and notice how often alliteration touches these too): "How to Talk to Your Teens," "How to Banish the Blues," "How to Get Your Husband to Dance,"

"How to Take a Daughter Shopping," "How to Cope with Criticism" (Norman Vincent Peale), "How to Help Your Husband Get Ahead (Stanley Schuler).

3. *Controversial titles*

These are generally titles which have shock value, either because they come out swinging against something a lot of people are already getting fed up with, or they take issue with a popular stand: "Don't Give Me Mother's Day," "I'm Sick of All This Sex," "Why I Deprive My Children" (Katherine Britton Mishler), "The PTA Is a Waste of Time" (William C. Kvaraceus), "Give Drugs to Addicts So We Can be Safe" (Jonah H. Goldstein), "Let's Stop Exalting Jerks" (Marya Mannes).

4. *Straight advice or statement titles*

Closely akin to the controversial is the title that simply states the premise in forthright terms. In these the words "do," "don't" or "why" frequently come in handy. Samples I've used for my articles are: "Marriage Isn't a Reform School," "Why Women Can't Talk to Their Husbands," "Why Husbands Can't Talk to Their Wives," "Don't Let People Monopolize You," "Don't be Afraid to be a Friend."

A quick trip through your current magazines will provide ample examples: "Try Everything Once" (William Moulton Marston in *The Rotarian*), "Why Roommates Make the Best Wives" (Joan Paulson, *Ladies' Home Journal*), "Make Room for the Simple Things" (Elizabeth Starr Hill in *Contemporary*) "If You're on a Diet, Shut Up!" (Harriet Van Horne, in *Redbook*).

5. *Question titles*

If stymied for a captivating title, put it in the form of a question: "Are You Training Your Daughter To Be a Wife?"

"Can Husbands and Wives Be Friends?" "Is All This Noise Necessary?" "What's Wrong with American Mothers?" "How Important Is Church?"

By using a "question" title, you also have an excellent cohesive device for the article itself. Put your opening statement in the form of this same question and deal with that question throughout the body of the article. You can then close the article by repeating the question and letting it summarize and clinch your conclusion. For instance: "How important is church? It helped us through the most critical time our family ever faced. It may well be the most important single force for hope and help for you too."

6. *A phrase or sentence*

A phrase makes a very attractive title. It may be a bit of dialogue taken directly from the article, it may be a single sentence. The phrase sometimes makes a longer title than is sometimes wished, but nonetheless it is effective—especially in nostalgia, or the personal essay: "All Doors Led to the Kitchen," "Every Child Was King in a Swing," "Golden Hours in Grandpa's Garden."

Or your phrase can be a bit of dialogue. For the article about older women and their spare time, I used the fancied quote: "Goodbye, Family, Hello, World!" In an article of a different type (being honest with children), "My Mother Is a Liar," seemed appropriate.

Or your phrase may be direct, succinct: "A Dad, a Boy, and a Car." Or it may answer the question posed: "Yes, We Do Marry Our In-Laws!" There are infinite possibilities for phrase titles in every article you do.

7. *First-person titles*

If you're writing a personal experience article your title should be no problem. "We Filmed Our Baby's Birth," "Our

Child Was a Runaway," "I Didn't Believe in God." Such titles provide instant impact. They ring true.

Whether the experience is as unique as crossing the Ganges on a crocodile, or as common as installment buying, such titles are attention-getting in their implied proclamation: "This happened to me and here's how I reacted. You'll find it significant too."

As in all other aspects of the creative article, title categories overlap. You'll find that the best ones contain several of the elements cited. Remember that good titles are lively, they have rhythm, and very often contain a vivid noun, adjective or action verb. Bad titles, on the other hand, are those which are vague, downbeat, innocuous, obtuse.

For instance: "Dread Is Inevitable," "The Rest of the Time," "I Shall Never Forget the Day," "Methods with Children That are Ineffective." Or those dry pedagogical titles that sound as if they had strayed from somebody's graduate thesis: "Marital Crises vs. Sibling Rivalry." They create the impression that here is a piece that is inept, tired, not quite with it. The writing which follows must be awfully good to overcome the handicap.

Think of your title as a banner—bright, new, snapping in the breeze, instead of a faded old one that wilts and sags and captures nobody's eye.

Quotes

Quotes are important extras for your creative article. So are the experiences and opinions of recognized authorities. They validate your arguments. They add both charm and substance. Mainly, they keep the whole article from sounding too "top of the head."

The creative article writer must fight a constant battle with his own ego. He is so fired with his own ideas it's hard to make room for anybody else's. Originally, I used to draw all my anecdotes from my own background. I either knew people to whom such things happened, or I made them up. I wrote and sold dozens of gay or impassioned articles without consulting references of any sort.

But all good things must end. *Better Homes and Gardens* had published a whole series of my articles on marriage and on child care when the editors got to matching notes one day and discovered I wasn't quoting anybody important. How come I, a mere housewife, presumed to know so much? Besides, all that money ought to be dug for a little harder. Hereafter would I please work in some authorities?

My first reaction was indignation: "People don't want a rehash of what a lot of other people think; they want to know what the author thinks!" It was with extreme annoyance that I trudged to the library to check out all the books they had on marriage. At first it was pretty dreary going; but I was promptly repaid by all the new article ideas that these more scholarly experts sparked.

Also, it was heartening to discover that many of my pet theories were validated by doctors, psychologists and marriage counselors. And to taste the excitement of the researcher when he finds something he's searching for! It was also startling, and valuable, to discover that there was a considerable body of opinion that disagreed with some of my arguments. (Here lay ammunition for that "anticipate your opposition" so important to the framework of any article of advice or controversy.) Finally, it made me think my ideas through more deeply.

I don't honestly think that the articles I wrote after this were that much better. But they were tailored to fit the growing demands that such articles "be authenticated and based on a firm ground of research." I made the transition in method by simply blocking out what I wanted to say anyway, then hunting until I found a suitable passage in a book or scholarly report which agreed with me.

Newspapers

I then discovered another excellent source of quotes: newspaper interviews. A celebrity comes to town, and his ideas on life, love, and his own success will make a news feature. Generally this person will relate anecdotes to illustrate how he got his start, or little incidents that influenced his philosophy. So here you have two possibilities: The quote that will simply flavor and underscore your point: "As Lauren Bacall once said, 'There's only one thing to do with life when it starts closing in on you—cope with it, dammit.' " Or the appropriate anecdote: "When Lauren Bacall was six years old her mother sent her to the neighborhood grocery for a pound of butter. It was a hot night, the butter melted, and by the time she got home she was smeared, and the neighbor kids laughed—"

Newspapers and their magazine sections are filled with such material. There are also profiles and full-length fact pieces about public personalities in magazines. And to get back to newspapers for a minute, don't overlook the obituaries. When a prominent figure dies his biography is dug out of the publisher's morgue and brought up to date. Generally this includes characteristic quips, statements and little stories.

Here, for instance, is part of a yellowed clipping from an AP dispatch on the death of Oscar Hammerstein:

> Mr. Hammerstein was an unabashed sentimentalist and made no bones about it. "I know the world is filled with trouble and many injustices," he once said. "But reality is as beautiful as it is ugly. I think it is just as important to sing about beautiful mornings as it is to talk about slums. I just couldn't write anything without hope in it."

Then followed an anecdote about the time Mae West advised him, "Kid, get out of the theatre and be a lawyer. The theatre isn't for you. You've got too much class." Watch for such material and when it strikes you, cut it out. File it with your folders of article ideas, or keep a celebrity file. Then when you need a quote or illustration for a special theme, you will have one.

Be a name-dropper

Name-dropping may not be good manners in conversation; in articles it's expected. All the names need not be world-famous, however. (In fact it's refreshing if they're not—you thereby avoid the overworked episodes and statements.) Almost any person who has gained distinction can be used as an authority: Bennetta Washington, wife of the first Negro mayor of the District of Columbia and an outstanding educator; Madame Alexander, who has been designing beautiful dolls for generations; Charles Ross Anthony, the poor Tennessee farm boy who founded the Anthony chain stores. The financial pages as well as the sports and cultural pages continually recount the stories of successful and significant people.

You can find another source of authorities among your own acquaintances. This is different from the "my child's teacher," "a neighbor," "a doctor friend" approach. To qualify that doctor as a genuine authority, you name him: "Dr. Jonathan Williams, internationally known neurosurgeon," "Hazel Wilson, author of children's books and critic for the Washington *Star*," "Erika Thieme, director of The Dance Theatre."

Almost any writer who socializes as he should knows some distinguished people. It's perfectly legitimate, and a great time saver, to use them. Simply pick up the phone and say: "I'm doing an article about the values of solitude, getting away from it all—what's been your experience, what do you think?" Or, "The other night at that party you were saying some interesting things about sex reform. May I quote you?" Or write a letter, giving a portion of your proposed text, and asking an opinion.

A final source of quotes lies in the classical reference. Every writer should have handy on his bookshelf a complete Shakespeare, the Bible, Emerson's essays, Lord Chesterfield's letters to his son, copies of Ruskin or other favorite philosophers, plus as many books of quotations as he can. Bartlett's is the best known, but there are countless others, some in paperback, some to be found in second hand bookstores. The beauty is that the quotations are generally organized alphabetically and by topic, and it's quite easy to find the perfect phrase.

They are used in this way: "As Victor Hugo said, 'To reform a man, you must begin with his grandmother'! And true, you can't hope to change basic traits. Nature has fixed those so firmly you must accept any individual pretty much as-is—" ("Marriage Isn't a Reform School") . . . Or, "Tolstoy declared, 'The woman who marries me must know my most secret thoughts,' and handed his bride his diary. A man as smart as Tolstoy should have known better." ("Do You Dare to Be Honest in Marriage?")

Getting permission

Now let's summarize the business of permissions:

1. Books

If you quote from a book, write publisher and/or author for permission. Short prose quotations used for illustration constitute "fair use", and permission need not be asked. But I think it both wise and courteous to give the title, author, and publisher's name in the text or in a footnote. Of course, books in "public domain" (not still protected by copyright) can be quoted without permission, but again the title, author, and publisher should be mentioned. Usually, I don't write for permission where necessary until the article has been accepted. (This saves embarrassment if the article does not make the grade.) What if permission is refused? This is not likely to happen very often, since publishers want as much mention of the books they publish as they can get. But if permission to quote is refused, of course you must not use the quote in question.

2. Published interviews

It is not strictly necessary to ask permission to quote published interviews which may be impossible to track down. Your newspaper clipping may be brittle with age (likewise the reporter) and may not even carry a byline. If a celebrity is quoted, "Life's tough. Take it," then those words are in the public domain. If, however, you want to use the anecdote of the melted butter from somebody's hard-won interview, I think you owe it to the original author (if you know who it is) to notify him: "That was a great interview; do you mind if I work it into my own article?"

If the author objects, you can always write to the subject himself and get the story. But some of my best friends are reporters, and I know how furious they get at having some of their material used by other fact writers whose products are sometimes merely clip and paste jobs. *Never* use another writer's words in retelling the anecdote.

Now if you want to quote from somebody's published speech —say the head of the mental clinic, who has addressed the Ki-Wives—write to the gentleman, himself, rather than to the reporter or newspaper who covered it. You will probably be rewarded by a complete copy of his text, plus other data, and will have made a friend.

3. Friends and acquaintances

Yes, you do have to get their permission to quote them by name—especially anyone in the medical profession. But generally they are flattered.

8

The Personal Article

It is almost impossible to separate the author from his material, whether he is writing fact or fiction. His attitude, viewpoint, and individuality cannot but influence both his choice of subject and the way he handles it. This is particularly true of the creative article. It is by its very essence, personal. But there are some approaches to it that are more definitely personal than others: The true experience. Articles on such subjects as marriage and parenthood. The personal essay or sketch. Nostalgia.

Since these last forms pose fewer problems, let's discuss them briefly first.

The short personal sketch

You simply dip into your own memories or daily experiences and activities and discover one moment, statement, action or object which seems to epitomize some universal theme. This may be even a time of day, as done so exquisitely by Jean Hersey in "Early Morning Magic" (*Woman's Day*):

> There is a stillness, a hush abroad as I touch the day at its beginning. Neighbors' houses are silent, no cars pass at the end of the lane. I hear the sound of a single bee among the marigolds, and somewhere a cardinal sings.

She then explores this hour at different seasons and places, bringing in all its rich imagery and wonder, to conclude:

A deep sense of oneness with nature and with all of living, a quickening, widens horizons and lifts me to reach beyond myself . . . I will hear a kind of song within that sings for hours or days and brings me secrets that do not fit into words.

Your sketch may be based upon a phrase that impressed you, an epigram or bit of philosophy which expresses some human wisdom for you in capsule form—anything so simple as a mother's constant reminder, "Shut the door!" I turned this into "Shut Those Doors Behind You" (on regret, missed opportunities, etc.), "the only doors that are important are those we open today." Or the familiar shout, "Mother, I'm home!" Tracing it from kindergarten, through college, into your children's marriages:

They grow up so fast; they go away one by one. After a while, only on visits does that glad cry come. . . . Home is somewhere else. A different job, a different life, a different love to follow yours, a different person to greet them when they return. . . .

And that once-familiar cry has taken on a new significance. . . . You don't have to worry. They have reached their destination. Each one is safely in. In a new and much more wonderful way, each voice is assuring you: "I'm home, Mother. I'm *home!*"

Your inspirational sketch may use a familiar object as its symbol. My friend, the radio commentator Ruth Wells, wrote a little gem called "The Cookie Jar" which won a national prize as best expressing American family tradition. In my column and magazine pieces, I have used a mother's apron, a father's wallet, the flag on the schoolhouse, a tent, a swing, a calendar, to clarify simple yet significant truths.

This, for instance, from "The Family Calendar" (*McCall's*):

What record will be written there before another year has passed? What shining events to be looked forward to? What trivial tasks dutifully cited; what joys, or sorrows? For the calendar that hangs in the kitchen is so much more than a sheaf of dates—it is your family's history.

Use familiar sights: Giving strangers directions. Seeing youngsters across a busy street. Writing "The Letter Home."

So women sit writing. Up and down the street, in the cities and the small towns, all over the world. Writing that diary of their destiny, making their entry into the account books of their lives: "Dear Folks—" "Dear Mother and Dad. . . ."

The entire essay is based upon a single analogy or bit of symbolism which is its own memory device. Thus unity is inherent, and with one incisive theme, you achieve one mood or tone, and one final effect. Sometimes it is written entirely in the first person, sometimes you step back a few paces to use the third person, or you may concentrate on the second person, "you." But the feeling is always first person, in other words, intimate.

The writing must be clear, pure, succinct. Sentiment is always present, but sentimentality, never. Once you spill over into clichés (Father's "care-worn hands," etc.) or anything that smacks of hearts and flowers, you're ruined. The writing must not only "give pleasure" (which Virginia Woolf considered one of the basic principles of the essay), it must have a certain timelessness: "A good essay must have this permanent quality about it; it must draw its curtain round us, but it must be a curtain that shuts us in, not out."

The only earthly way to learn to write essays is to write them! Don't strive for perfection at first; just pour your essay ideas into your notebook as they come to you, and let them age a bit. Meanwhile, study the published essays to soak up their flavor, their rhythms, their delicate balance of ideas, emotion and phrase. Then go back to your own earlier sketches and polish until they shine.

Nostalgia

There are several things to bear in mind when writing nostalgia:

Be accurate.

Don't try to cram too much into any one article.

Make your material applicable to as many people as possible.

Don't look *too* far back; you'll sound really doddering, and younger readers won't bother with you. Besides giving away your age—you'll have a hard time selling the article. In one I described how housewives beat their rugs and swept with brooms. When an editor objected that this sounded a little too primitive, I hastened to add that Mother *had* a vacuum, but it was always breaking down and she didn't really trust it; besides, any woman of muscle and gumption felt more virtuous coping with dirt the hard way.

There is also the danger of sounding too much like a has-been. I get long, delightful letters from elderly people who think I'm their contemporary. Or they say, "You must be much younger than I am, how can you remember flatirons and silent movies?"

Well, I've ironed many a brother's shirt with flatirons heated on the family coal stove and vividly remember silent movies, and the exciting advent of sound. But I am careful to include the fact that I am still the mother of teen-agers, who make the contrast between today's entertainment and the pure fare of those days more keen; for a nostalgic article ought to be something more than a picture of the good old days. It should say something, I think, about the current scene.

Your memories must be accurate. Who was President when we sat munching popcorn during the Pathé newsreel? And *was* Pathé the name? Did Lindbergh fly the Atlantic before or after Rudy Vallee hit the scene with his megaphone? When in doubt, be sure to check. I don't want any reader to crow over my errors (as readers are prone to do); worse, I don't want to irritate them, as I am irritated when I find mistakes in a published piece.

These articles do not require a lot of research; they are about as "top of the head" as you can get. But when you do mention persons or trade names, make absolutely sure they could have been on the scene.

I've already mentioned focusing on *one* aspect of the past: the old-fashioned kitchen, children's games, the mail order catalogs. This gives unity, and keeps you from dragging in everything you happen to recall. However, as you describe the various aspects of your subject, naturally you mention the incidental props, which also contribute to a picture of the period. In "All Doors Led to the Kitchen," for example, that big, warm, "first family room," the kitchen, is not only furnished in detail, down to the drip pan under the ice box, but we learn something else:

> Hearing the jingle of harness or plod of hooves up the shady street, Mother would open the top lid, make a quick inspection, and send one of us out to tell Johnny Peterson how many pounds today. The Petersons were a big German family who drove teams onto the frozen lake and hewed the ice with giant saws. Their castle-high ice houses were landmarks along the windy shore.
>
> Other kids would already be swarming the hooded wagon, begging bright slivers and chunks to suck . . . Grabbing a block with the jaws of his mighty tongs, Johnny would haul it toward him and split it cleanly with a pick . . . Then "slosh" went his bucket of water to rinse the sawdust off, and he'd heave it to his shoulder and stagger, a kind of Atlas, toward the house.

After supper, when the dishes were washed, the dishpan hung on its nail on the back porch, the family gathered around the kitchen table to eat popcorn and play Flinch, Old Maid, or Rummy—although preachers still thundered against "cards" and Mother was uneasy about this wickedness.

The vantage point remains the kitchen, but from it we see other details of a bygone era.

Finally, a nostalgic article cannot be simply the author's egoistic outpourings of his personal reminiscences. Even though written in first person, with points enlivened by anecdotes of friends and family, paradoxically it must not be a mishmash of folksy tales interesting only to the persons involved. It must be sufficiently general to open the gates of memory to others, to make them exclaim, "That's just how it was. Why, I recall—". Very often readers write to you in this vein, adding such wonderful material of their own that ideas for new articles are generated.

Personal experience

Magazines are publishing more true first-person stories than ever before. Editors have come to recognize that the most valid truths, as well as the most interesting adventures, are those that come straight out of human experience. This form of the creative article is by far your best bet. The trick, however, is in the telling.

Good Housekeeping speaks of its audience of "average families," and warns, "Most writers miss the boat because of lack of impact, warmth and dramatic appeal with which the average housewife can identify." In short, the material itself may be so unique and dramatic that it commands attention; or it may be a fairly common experience which *becomes* dramatic in the telling. In either case, it must be so written that the average person can relate to it.

By drama the last thing we mean is heaving bosoms and scalding tears, posturings, pantings, mad dashes for freedom; voices that beg, scream, implore, whine, shout, or any of the paraphernalia of action or emotion that bespeaks *melodrama*. Drama is simply the ability to portray a believable character, and to let the reader share that character's experience in the most intensely interesting and beneficial way.

This often means adopting the techniques used in fiction: suspense, threat, rising drama, moment of truth, and sometimes denouement.

One major difference between fiction and the personal experience article is in characterization. *You* (or people very close to you) are the major character; hence you cannot or need not give much of a physical description. Never, heaven forbid, use the "My mirror told me I was beautiful," approach; nor, "I am a tall, husky specimen with curly blonde hair," although little graphic touches can sometimes be worked in—"It was a big load even for my six foot, two-hundred-pound frame—" When well done these touches can help the reader to visualize, and they may be necessary sometimes to clarify the action.

Generally speaking, there is seldom need to go deeply into motivation; and there is simply no time, and rarely much reason, to flash back into a lot of biographical data to establish character. You are simply onstage, and character is implicit in the way you handle, react to, and resolve the situation you describe.

Furthermore, the character is always subordinate to the experience. You are not Exhibit *A*; you are merely the vehicle for Exhibit *A* (the experience). This is in contrast to the fact article, wherein a prominent or interesting personality is presented. The author interviews his subject, gathers all possible data about him, and draws his portrait for the public. Or the subject himself talks about himself, within a question-and-answer framework, an "as told to" article, or if he can actually write, he may even produce his own self-revelations.

In the creative type of personal experience article, however, the character is genuinely moved or changed or affected in some way by the experience. And this prospect of *change* (opinion altered, lesson learned, etc.) is usually evident from the very beginning:

> As a child growing up by the edge of the sea, I used to wonder about the people who, on a mild summer's day, somehow managed to drown. . . . On Tuesday, September 20, 1966, I learned that there is no special trick to drowning. Anyone can do it. Even a strong swimmer like myself—
> ("But We're Alive!", Doris Agee, *Reader's Digest*)

> Two years after the death of my husband, Dr. Paul Carlson, I returned to Africa. Going back to anything or to any place after one has been away involves emotional risk. This is true even when

the parting has been a happy one and not the result of shattering tragedy as was mine.

("Congo Revisited," by Lois Carlson, in *Christian Herald*)

Bob and I became engaged quietly last New Year's Eve. It was just about the *last* quiet moment we were to enjoy for the next five months.

"It Was a Beautiful Wedding, But—" Janet McGregor, *Good Housekeeping*)*

On the other hand, the narrator's original concepts may be only more firmly established by the adventure he describes. In "Why We Sold the Farm" (*Farm Journal*), H. Gordon Green relates the trials of small farming—hard work, low income—which drove him to cash in on the land while the price was right, only to discover that both he and the family had lost so many other values (good neighbors, the rewards of working with animals) that he rushed right out and bought a bigger farm!

(Note the *comparison and contrast* in all these examples.)

A definite fictional technique found in most good personal experience articles is suspense. And one technique of suspense is to hint at a threat, suggest impending danger, or sometimes disappointment or frustration, then build gradually up to it. (Delay the onrushing car; leave the time-bomb ticking; turn away from the poor guy who's just bet his last two bucks on a horse that can't—or can he?—win.)

Suspense is implicit in the opening of "But We're Alive!" (You are about to share with me the experience of nearly drowning . . . wait, I'll tell you how it came about.) It is evident in the apprehension felt by Mrs. Carlson, the missionary's wife about to return to the scene of her husband's murder. There is suspense even in the portent of trouble from commercial interests when an engagement is announced: "At times I envisioned bankruptcy for my father, nervous collapse for my mother, and a deterioration of my own marriage before it had even begun . . . yet in the beginning, on that magical New Year's Eve—"

Suspense is not always a matter of delay. It can be attained

by a simple narration of a situation which itself is threatening
or exciting:

> I was surf fishing in Bungalow Inlet, Virginia, when the rod
> suddenly came alive in my hands. I could barely keep it from
> being torn from my grasp.
> ("Sharks, Anyone?" by Zack Taylor in *Sports Afield*.)

And whether the "adventure" be as unusual as hauling in a
shark or as ordinary as getting married, the articles have in
common a sense of universal truth. During the ordeal of nearly
drowning, Doris Agee has learned: "In the future I will swim
—and live—with new respect for the forces of nature." She
has realized too the unutterable preciousness of the little things
in life: "Because I came so close to losing them, I can never
again take them for granted."

Lois Carlson returns spiritually strengthened by her sad
journey: "Because the doctor died, people have had their eyes
opened. We don't need to be afraid any more." . . . Janet
McGregor decides she should have taken her dad's advice and
eloped. . . . Zack Taylor discovers his own stamina in coping
with the monster shark.

This is what keeps the personal experience article from being
a mere first-grade exercise of Show and Tell. The author is
not merely showing off; he is showing what he has gained in
understanding, saying something worthwhile to the reader, in
addition to relating the tale itself.

Writing about marriage

The relationship between men and women is the oldest and
surely the most fascinating subject in the world. I always tell
my classes, "Get the words Man, Woman, Husband, Wife,
Love, Marriage, or Sex into the title if you can. They always
get attention."

In writing about marriage, however, the average person is

up against tough competition from the experts; sometimes
psychologists, psychiatrists, marriage counselors even serve on
the magazine's staff. The way many free-lance writers get
around this is to team up with an authority and co-sign the
article; or they take a topic and quote the expert at length. For
me this is not writing a creative article in the true sense. To
write a creative article about marriage is to convey your ideas
on the subject and quote the professionals in the field to con-
firm them.

It is quite possible for a writer to do a lot of reading in the
area, arm himself with the necessary authorities, marshal his
anecdotes and case histories, and come up with an excellent
piece. But more often than not, it will be your own experience
which has inspired the idea in the first place. It is this fundamental slant or concept that gives your article focus, and which
lends conviction to the tone and style.

There is, in fact, something very appealing about a frank,
curbstone opinion, presented without apology, provided, of
course, it is presented *well*. When I was first feeling my way,
I came across an article written in this vein which impressed
me. I failed to save it and can't remember who wrote it or where
it appeared, but I do remember the special charm of its innocent: "I am just a housewife. I have no advanced degrees,
and I barely squeaked through college. But I have been married ten years and feel I know a little something about the
business of getting along with *any*one to whom you've com-
mitted your life."

I am paraphrasing roughly, but her words were brisk, well
chosen, and her arguments persuasive. Other women could
identify with her from the opening shot, and would listen to
what she had to say. I don't know whether that writer ever
produced another article, but I do know that the sheer vigor
and candor of her approach impressed me and helped me to
produce mine. It dawned on me that anyone who writes sufficiently well and has something to say is entitled to be heard.

There are real and ever-present dangers, however, in drawing too closely upon your own experiences. As I have stated, more editors are asking for the "This happened to me" type article. First-person accounts that once appeared primarily in the confessions now make the covers of some of the formerly pristine slicks. "His Mistress Saved Our Marriage," "Our Experiment With Group Sex." That kind of thing. If you are impelled to write the intimate details of a serious marital problem, no matter how vital and helpful your solution to it, it seems to me that good taste and common sense decree that it be anonymous, or signed with a pseudonym. In the first place, a writer should not be an exhibitionist. In the second, merely belonging to this hallowed profession gives the writer no moral right to embarrass the other people who are inevitably involved.

Unless it is treated humorously, this applies even to marriage relationships less grim. I had one shattering experience. I did an article which I called, "What Every Woman Wants" (affection, attention, romance). I contrasted the basic attitude men and women have toward marriage, and discussed and amply illustrated feminine disillusionment when romantic attentions dwindle. Just in case anybody got the idea I was criticizing my own husband, however, I threw in: "My own mate is, thank heaven, a shining exception to all this."

Imagine my shock, then, when the article appeared as, "What Became of the Man I Married?" A terrific title, yes, but very unfair to my husband, or so it seemed to me. He took it like the good sport he is, but I was devastated. Partly to get myself off the hook, I wrote a follow-up article showing the other side of the coin and calling it, "What Became of the Girl *You* Married?" Both articles made *Reader's Digest* and received world-wide circulation.

Here again we see how there are at least two articles in almost every one you write. You simply look at the other side of the question, the opposition viewpoint, which you have been careful to include, and build it up into a new piece to rebut and balance the one you wrote before. This is not hypocrisy or

even ambivalence; it is merely playing fair. And the ability
to do this relieves you of the hazard of being *over*-personal in
writing about anything so personal as marriage.

I have written dozens of articles without including my husband except in the most casual or inferential way. This is for
the further, very important, reason that there is something
offensive about using your own relationship as the good example, and something even more offensive about using it as a bad
one! By the same token, I have written a number of articles
about in-laws without ever referring to mine.

If you write with any force, the reader can tell that you've
been through things and know what you are talking about.

In dealing with marriage, as with any other subject, the
writer must keep up to date. The old-fashioned problems will
always be with us, but they have to be presented in the light of
the current scene. One issue of *New York* Magazine reflects the
new look in male-female teaming: "The Crisis of the Couple,"
"Can Couples Survive?" "Videotaping Your Marriage to Save
It," "Moving In—The Logistics of Living Together." People
are living together without benefit of matrimony ("*What* benefit?" they demand). Women's libbers claim that "wife" is another word for slave. Communes and group marriages exist; the
best seller *Open Marriage* opened a great many mental and emotional doors.

Such changes may be deplored, but cannot be ignored. Not
if you wish to sell and to be heard.

Writing about parents and children

The subject of your progeny is also a highly personal one.
As writers we can approach it from two directions—or divide
it into two categories: parenthood itself, or child care.

In the first, we find such titles as: "The Decline and Fall
of the American Father," "The Missing American Mother,"
"Don't Blame Your Parents," "The Vanishing American

Father," "A Vote Against Motherhood," "Our Child Was a
Run-Away."

Whether the article be an intensely personal experience, as
in the last title, controversial protest as in "Don't Blame Your
Parents," or "A Vote Against Motherhood," or the social phe-
nomenon of fathers and mothers too busy to be home, the
subject under discussion is the *adult*. We are analyzing ourselves, rather than throwing a specific spotlight on the children.
This kind of article is found more often in general circulation
magazines than is the article about how to raise children. Some
very funny articles about the business of being a parent are
also published here—some tender sketches, some thoughtful
essays, out of which words of advice pertinent to children (if
only implied) will come. But in general, the emphasis is on
parents themselves.

In the other category, child-rearing, we face somewhat the
same problem as in writing about marriage. Some magazines
have their own child care departments. Others will buy only
from people with advanced degrees, or nurses, sociologists, or
others whose profession deals with children. A few seldom,
if ever, use the article of specific advice about children. Those
which do use them don't care who writes them, as long as they
are well done and have a real contribution to make.

Parents' Magazine, reflecting its own apt and time-honored
title, uses articles by recognized authorities, but also sometimes
uses contributions from parents who know whereof they speak
(provided they speak *well*—in other words write professionally). There is also a healthy crop of small magazines, aimed at
new or expectant mothers and fathers, which welcome their experiences. Some of these are sponsored by diaper services or
baby-products firms. They don't pay much, but are a good
place for beginners to try their wings. Most will send you free
sample copies if you ask. And so will most of the religious publications, which also use articles about home and family with
an upbeat or spiritual slant. Request a sample and study it be-

fore you submit. There are differences in style.

I can't stress too strongly that such publications are the best possible way to break into print—for pay. Any writer with both talent and children can do it if he (more likely she) is willing diligently to try.

Here too you must ask, however, how much of myself and my own family is it good to use? The answer depends upon the kind of article you are writing, and whether or not there is any-thing in your examples that could possibly hurt your youngster.

Obviously, if you are writing for *Baby Talk,* you can be as personal as you please. The baby couldn't care less! But I think you have to be wary about using your own children, even as the subject of humorous articles. Especially teen-agers. I have tremendous respect for the late Betty MacDonald, one of the funniest women ever to touch a typewriter. But I hope that her daughters were safely married when the story of their adolescence, *Onions in the Stew,* was published. Or that the author did a lot of camouflaging.

I feel so strongly about this that I once returned a thousand-dollar check rather than revise an article which the editor wanted me to make "more personal." It was about the tribula-tions, sometimes hilarious, sometimes anguishing, that beset a family when a boy comes down with "car-itis." I simply could not bring myself to name the boy, and pin his father to the mat; it just was not worth it. (I had written the article in terms of any typical family, using the second person "you." They wanted me to make it "I" and describe definite events. The article was eventually published, after their editing, but under a pseudonym.)

I may be unduly sensitive on this point, but I avoid this even with younger children, getting around it in columns and articles by trying never to refer to an actual child by name or age. Substituting "the youngest, the older boy, the middle one, our teen-ager," or some such term. Also, I almost never use any current, easily recognized example, lest it backfire at school.

Even so innocent an adventure as clumsily trying to help our Bluebird make a blanket roll for camp had repercussions. It seemed harmless and amusing when it appeared in my column, where the child's well-meaning teacher spied it, and had the mistaken judgment to read it to the class. Our little girl came home in tears: "They laughed at me!" she wailed.

Here your notebook proves invaluable. Write down the anecdotes, situations or problems as they occur, but postpone using them until the child is beyond caring, or sees their value and humor himself. Or at least until you can figure out a way to camouflage them, or utilize them without upsetting anyone.

Now this does not mean that you can't *really* write, at least along this line, until the kids grow up. (That's all too common an excuse for procrastination.) I have written and sold dozens of child-centered articles with my own children all over the place. It all depends on the *kind* of article you are writing, and your approach to it.

For instance, "How to Help Your Child Conquer Fear" is opened with an anecdote, a daughter's dancing across a footbridge with a harmless green snake coiled around a stick. And *my* impulse to scream and run. But how I overcame it, so as not to inflict my own tormenting snake fears on her. The article then discusses other foolish fears that parents pass along to their offspring; or shows by example how to protect them from such fears:

> A child should not only begin life sleeping alone in a darkened room, he should be taught the quiet loveliness of night. My husband used to turn out the lights and sit by a window with our toddler. "We can see the stars better this way. I can just barely see you—can you see me?" he'd laugh. . . . Such happy associations make the dark a friend.
>
> I don't mean to imply that we are model parents on this, or any other, score. It was sheer exasperation over too many nightly trips to the bathroom that inspired us to put a lamp on our daughter's bedside table when she was three. After that, proudly, and without qualms, she turned on her lamp, and trotted down the hall.

The above passage also shows something about tone. You must never sound like a "know-it-all": "We are not model parents . . . It was sheer exasperation." Note, too, the past tense: "My husband used to. . . . When our child was three." And it seemed in better taste not to specify a name.

A wrong or unfair approach to the same subject might have been handled like this: "Our daughter, Janie, 5, is absolutely terrified of everything that creeps or crawls. She has tantrums, she kicks and screams. I am determined that she overcome this." (Pretty bad, but what I am indicating is that the child is portrayed as the problem, the author as the wise heroine.) Or take the later incident of the dark: "Janie, I am proud to say, turns on her own light when she has to go to the bathroom at night, and marches herself down the hall." To use a child's name, present tense, about this particular function is just— well, not very good judgment.

It is also quite possible, often preferable, to write on these subjects without using your own children at all. Another article of mine, "Help Your Children to Like People," opens:

> The average American parent is eager to give his offspring the so-called advantages. We expose them to dancing lessons, scurry them to the best skin doctors when the bumps of adolescence appear . . . But too many of us neglect to equip our children with the greatest social advantage of all—the simple, old-fashioned virtue of learning to *like* people.

A number of suggestions follow, enumerated, and presented in statements like: "*Be a good example.* . . . Sons and daughters are but two-legged mirrors of ourselves. *Teach them that friends are worth forgiving.* 'I hate Johnny, I'm never going to play with him again!' Or, 'I'm not stopping by for Ruth any more, we're through!' are not unusual declarations in any household."

There are all sorts of ways to write beautifully, sensitively, helpfully about children. Owenita Sanderlin does it this way for *Parents' Magazine*, and for *Catholic Digest* in "The Wonderful Age of Four":

A four-year-old is somebody special. Not quite a baby and not quite a real little boy or girl, not quite a cherub and not quite an imp, his innocence is wondrous and his wisdom appalling!

In *Petroleum Today*, Edith Hunter describes her eight-year-old Charles, and his summer-long "service station," whose opening had to be postponed to accommodate the robins and rabbits that took refuge among his racks . . . In "Hey, Mom, Did You Bring Me a Present?" for *Woman's Day*, Jean Bradford uses the direct approach:

> I'm sure there must be other mothers besides me who have discovered that this Mom-what-did-you-bring-me business can be overdone. The fun goes out of it for both parent and child when the surprise turns out . . . to be a dud . . . Eventually I stumbled on a new approach that led me far away from the toy counters—

"We Like Bikes!" by Jean R. Komaiko, in *Parents' Magazine*, describes how a son's suggestion led to fun for the whole family:

> On a spring day three years ago my small son ran out of comrades. "Mom," said Bill, "the kids are busy and Debby won't ride with me. Why don't you borrow her bike and let's. . . . In a weak . . . moment I consented to my first bike ride in eighteen years. I've been cycling merrily ever since . . .

There are, in short, countless methods whereby you can explore the field of parent-child relationships with charm and tact, while making a real contribution.

Remember that the personal article, whatever its type, is a vehicle for communication. Which is, in essence, a matter of reader participation. Through you the reader himself must be caught up in the mainstream of living, and feel that he too has lived and learned.

9

Writing Humor

I have no business trying to tell anybody how to write humorous articles. Mine aren't funny enough to stand as humorous pieces in themselves. *I* think they're funny, some editors think they're funny—but not many think they're *that* funny, and I have sold only a few in that category. But humor keeps popping up in my articles, and I can recognize a genuinely funny piece in print or manuscript.

A touch of humor is just one of those little extras that brighten up an article and help it sell. But this humor must come naturally, otherwise the strain will show. Your article will become self-consciously cute or embarrassing. It will make the reader feel like the wife who has to sit politely smiling while her husband prances around in a lady's hat, or lengthily tells a not very funny story. Or like the class that sits groaning while their staid professor tosses off an old chestnut.

Which brings me to my first don't: *Don't* ever use an old joke (or even one currently making the rounds) in your article, under the impression that this is humorous writing. Occasionally even good writers who should know better are guilty of such attempts to "be funny," and I always wince for them. There is something about the very word or framework of a "joke" when reduced to print, which makes it suddenly dead. But a joking or kidding *attitude* toward your material is something else. You are personally amused by it as you write, and that amusement shines through.

You hit upon a usable pun which not only adds a flicker of fun, but doubles your meaning: "Delirium tree-trimmins" (Chester Goolrick in *Rural Living*), "Love and Hisses," (Charlie Rice's *Punchbowl*), "Hello, Dali!" (Will Stanton, *Contemporary*).

Seeking to avoid clichés, you give them a twist and get something very gay: "The Face Isn't Familiar Either," Philip Wylie. "A funny thing happened to me on my way through middle age," Richard Gehman. "Santa's bag is empty, and I'm left holding it," Corey Ford.

In trying to make up original analogies and allusions, choose those which will give your writing a comic bounce, even if you are writing a serious article. For instance, when I was writing about the bad influence immoral movies may have on young people and the paltry defenses of the public against them, I stated, "Attempting to combat the sex tycoons with such weapons is like aiming a pea shooter at a bull elephant." I tried several figures before that one struck me. It was just ludicrous enough to say what I intended.

Here's an example from "Marriage Isn't a Reform School": "Kiss the girl or boy of your dreams goodbye. You're not married to Enzio Pinza—or Dagmar; you're married to just plain Bill or Jane Jones." (That shows how long ago that article was written. If it hadn't sold and I was trying to revise it, I would choose current entertainers; even in love symbols, styles change.)

And, again, from "Do You Dare To Be Honest in Marriage?": "Practically all wives fudge a little when it comes to what they pay for things." (I'm using intentional vernacular, bordering on cliché, here, to make it all sound very homely and everyday.) "What woman in her right mind ever admits to buying a dress that wasn't marked down? And it's sheer unconscious feminine psychology to add anything from $10 to $50 to what it was marked down *from*. Any man who has any wits about him at all knows she does this, comes to expect it, and almost certainly would be faintly shocked if she didn't."

This is not outright humor in the Jane Goodsell, Erma Bombeck, or Peg Bracken sense. But it's humorous in attitude, in tone. It bespeaks a cheerful approach to a subject that might well have been treated with dead seriousness, and is, in other places in the article. It is the light treatment that editors like.

You must be careful, however, that your light or comic touches occur in just the right places, and do not spoil that so very important tone. Here is an example of misplaced, woefully inappropriate humor:

> These thugs attacked without provocation, they were suddenly upon me and I was fighting for my very life. Their blows rained down, they were trying to stamp upon me. "Father forgive them," I prayed even in that moment. And I was in dead earnest, in fact I was nearly dead, Ernest, as my brother used to quip.

The reader, like the victim, rolls his eyes to heaven. It is not only an antique joke, but is worse—it injects a screechingly wrong note.

Timing and beat

Timing is tremendously important. One of my brothers was in show business, and I learned from him how comics must develop a perfect sense of timing: The pause before the punchline, the quick pickup, the delicate balance between getting a laugh and laying an egg.

This timing, this complete command of pace, is especially important to the writer, whether he's writing straight humor or material that is humorous in approach. He must phrase and rephrase, add and subtract, until the episode or reference balances out to achieve its funniest impact. In most instances it is the subtracting that helps most. The wisecrack *must* crack— and then quit right there. The anecdote cannot lumber on for pages. Pare the dialogue until every line is funny, or leads into the next line, which will be. Avoid pointless chatter like this:

> "I don't like this," said my wife, pouting.
> "Well, it can't be helped, honey," I told her, grinning slyly.

"It can too. You could do something about it if you would. I declare I never knew anybody to be so contrary. Why, sometimes I think you haven't a brain in your head."

"Oh, come now, you don't think that, you can't, after all you married me. Now let's see what we can do . . ."

On and on, wasting the reader's time until finally a bright line is painfully squeezed out.

On the other hand, it is the deft, subtle little balances of "he said," or "the child remarked, grinning up at me," that give your comedy the exact *beat*, the pace, the timing to amuse the mental ear. A good way to test yourself about this is to try to write some anecdotes for "Life in These United States" or squibs for other departments in *Reader's Digest*. Read yours aloud, and then read their published ones aloud, and *listen*. See how yours compare. It is not easy to compress an experience into a paragraph or to combine a few words in a way that packs a wallop.

Genuine humorists usually have this intuitive sense of timing. This is why stand-up comedians can tell a joke and have the audience in tears of laughter, while the less gifted may tell the same story and have people groaning. Those who have to labor to be the life of the party usually aren't. But writing humor also requires work and practice. The writers don't just take dictation from gag writers, but may rewrite a situation or revise a sentence half a dozen times before it feels or sounds right.

Logic

Oddly enough, humor, which depends so frequently upon hyperbole, has its own stubborn logic. It must be based upon reason and reality, life as we actually know it to be. The contrast may be one of the psychological reasons it strikes us funny.

Let me try to make this clear: A long time ago, when my efforts to make money through writing included soap contests, limericks and light verse, I also wrote gag lines for a cartoonist.

One, I blush to admit, suggested an escaped convict at a fancy party, saying, "Oh, yes, I'm sought after everywhere." The artist shot it back with this comment: "If he were being sought by the police, he could not possibly be at this party. Be logical —humor is based on logic."

I never forgot that advice. The more logical, the more reasonable the humorist is, the funnier his flights of exaggeration. You know he's kidding, but somewhere down below his wildest fancies lies this hard core of truth. This is what made "Be the First on Your Block to Own a Ton of Steel" so hilarious. This could happen (and in this instance did happen) if a reasonable guy decided to promote such an unorthodox deal.

It is why articles about housekeeping and children and husbands by Erma Bombeck are always funny; they are based upon perfectly natural, logical home situations. She just soups them up and turns the penetrating light of her gay logic upon them. It is why Fletcher Cox, writing in the small journal *Rural Living* (published by the Association of Electric Cooperatives), is funny when he describes a day he is impelled to challenge all the pointless bits of conversation people exchange.

When the bank teller asks, "How are you?" he asks, "Do you mean mentally or physically?" When a guy says, "See you, Fletch, take it easy," he responds, "What do you mean? When will you see me, and take *what* easy?" And, again, he counters, "Oh, I'll see you around," with "Around *where*?"

This isn't hilarious; it's just low key humor, but amusing because it is so familiar, and so absolutely *logical*. Mr. Cox is forcing us to look at our common absurdities, and tracking them to their logical (if *un*familiar) conclusion.

The would-be humorist often isn't logical. He seems to think that sheer unmotivated nuttiness is enough. I recently read a book-length manuscript for a publisher in which the basic set-up could have been insanely funny. The treatment made it merely insane. In addition to many other defects, it lacked this essential logic. The hero was determined to operate a very unusual business from the White House. (In fairness to the author and his excellent idea I won't tell you what it was.) Complication piled upon ludicrous complication. Yet it was never clearly established how the man and his family actually got there, or what their motivations were. Most of the comedy collapses because it has no logical foundation, even in basic character. The reader keeps wondering how the incidents *could* be happening in the first place, and since this is never revealed, credibility is destroyed. They just couldn't have happened that way.

Here we see again how closely the creative article writer is kin to the fiction writer. Particularly the humorist. Whether writing a short piece for *The New Yorker,* any popular magazine, or a funny book, he must understand what motivates human behavior; his characters must be soundly conceived. Then when they behave in a strange fashion the reader will know why, and his credulity will not be strained.

Hyperbole

Hyperbole, or the art of exaggeration, is the humorist's meat. He takes a perfectly plausible situation and blows it to preposterous proportions. Or he takes some fantastic possibility and makes it seem ridiculously reasonable. Art Buchwald and Alan King are masters of this.

Take Alan King's witty satire on physical fitness in *McCall's,* "Fit for What?":

So what are we preparing our children for? Are we planning to *wrestle* the Communists? . . .

Both my sons can do twenty push-ups without straining, but they haven't got enough energy to pick their clothes up off the floor. They can do sit-ups all day, but haven't the strength to walk to school . . . In fact, out where I live, they don't *learn* to walk until they're nineteen. Any kid worth his salt drives to school in his own car—and when I say "car" I don't mean a family cast-off or secondhand jalopy. The youngster with last year's model parks it three blocks from school and slinks the rest of the way in shame.

Elinor Goulding Smith uses similar exaggeration (minus the sardonic note) in "How I Manage to Make the Best Possible Dinner in the Whole Wide World" (*Family Circle*):

> In the aisles . . . women eye shelves and slump over baskets in attitudes of utter dejection. Some give anguished groans, their hands trembling as they brush the hair from their brow, muttering despairingly to the world at large, *"What* shall I have for dinner tonight?"
>
> I don't do *that* . . . I have a method I have perfected over a period of 20 years, and at last I am ready to share it with the world . . . I plant myself firmly in front of the store manager, and say in a clear executive voice, *"Tell* me what to have for dinner tonight!"* . . . I'll be your slave for three weeks. Four? Six? I'll wash your car, shovel your driveway.

The entire article is one hilarious blow-up of the problem every housewife faces every day: What to have for dinner?

You will recognize in all successful hyperbole a basis of absolute logic and truth. That's exactly what makes it so funny. From this base of all too familiar experience, we love to be catapulted into its extremes.

A word of caution, however. Hyperbole is not to be confused with hysteria. Verbs of intense emotion or exaggerated action do not in themselves make humor; such words as "scream," "stamp," "smirk," "leer," etc. are to be used sparingly.

Self-satire

A staple on the shelves of humor is the article of self-satire. You simply take some foible, weakness, or other aspect of your own personality, and make fun of it. Your helplessness before almost any of the things other people seem to manage:

> Few people will accept the cold, somber, and often appalling fact about me; I cannot remember names and I cannot remember faces, either. ("The Face Isn't Familiar Either," Philip Wylie, *Suburbia Today*.)

The subject of weight is always good for a laugh, and humor is the approach used by Katherine Hillyer here:

It is said that the thin rats bury the fat rats, but I no longer care. I just hope they break their nasty little toothpick arms burying lovable fat old me. ("The Whole World Is Going to Love Fat Old Me," Katherine Hillyer, in *Good Housekeeping*)*

Self-satire is, itself, filled with hyperbole. Generally, you belittle yourself; or you may brag about yourself (as in Elinor Goulding Smith's formula for cooking "The Best Possible Dinner in the Whole Wide World"); sometimes you pretend to be protesting the traits of somebody else, but the last laugh is always on you. "The Things My Wife Drags Home!" which John G. Hubbell deplores in *Christian Herald,* all turn out to be highly original home additions, or priceless antiques. Or again, you make yourself the fall guy for some common, incurable trait, such as "My Wife Doesn't Understand Me!" (because she won't shut up and listen) by Ralph E. Barber, in *Lady's Circle.* "What bugs me and every other happy-go-lucky husband willing to accept the carload of faults that comes with the small fraud known as a bride is that she *could* understand if she only *would*." But despite his merry mournings, you get a picture of a terrific gal putting up with *him*.

This sort of thing looks easy. It isn't. There is the ever-present danger of straining for effect, or of sounding just too, too cute. Once you turn the spotlight on yourself, even in a manner meant to be unflattering, the audience expects you to be very entertaining indeed to compensate for the attention you're getting. This is the trouble with many amateur attempts. When coyness is substituted for cleverness, the result is only embarrassing:

I'll betcha you're beginning to think I'm just about the worst steno' in the world. Well, I betcha you could just about be right, on account of I could hardly barely get through shorthand, and my typing, goodness! As for spelling, silly as it may sound, sometimes I can't really remember how to spell my own name. Well, but this boss (poor man) decided to take a chance (he was sooo good looking too) maybe because I batted my new false eyelashes at him.

Goodness!

Humorous protest

Very funny articles can evolve from taking a popular concept and burlesquing it. You are objecting to something, and your objection may actually be quite sincere, but the whole thing is done with tongue in cheek. Katherine Hillyer's self-satire above is also a slap at the constant emphasis on dieting. She just decided to take a self-kidding, humorous approach to convey her strong opinions on the subject.

There are other ways of doing it. Jane Goodsell's "Women Never Nag!" (*The American Weekly*) wades into the cliché about nagging wives, and declares that what we need is *more* nagging from this front. Husbands do it, children do it all the time:

> Insurance salesmen hound you. . . . Vacuum cleaner salesmen won't take no for an answer. . . . Everybody nags but women. It isn't fair!

Ralph Schoenstein's "Merrily We Probe Along" (*Saturday Evening Post*) deplores the vogue for psychiatry:

> People who'd always thought they were happy are suddenly learning how sick they are. "You poor fool, how can you dare tell me you're happy when you haven't even been analyzed?"

And here is an absolute classic of this genre which I once clipped from *The American Mercury*. Doris McFerran's "For God and the Kiddies," which comes on strong and swinging:

> For two years I earned my living from God and the kiddies. I wrote for the Sunday School magazines. I suppose you'll tell me there are harder ways to make a living. How would I like to be a ditch-digger, for instance, or one of the fellows who keeps the

geography textbooks up to date? Well, give me a shot at either of those jobs and watch me pitch in. But take, oh take, those kids away!

You'll notice that these examples, like almost every form of humor, are rich in hyperbole.

Humorous specifics

You will also find that genuinely amusing articles make liberal use of that extra discussed earlier, Specifics. Definite details, which are sometimes funny in themselves.

This from Shirley Jackson's "Mother, Honestly!" (*Good Housekeeping*)*:

> Take that woman you noticed the other day, just sitting by herself over a cup of coffee, staring straight ahead. Or trying to exchange a pair of size 16 subteen Bermuda shorts for a size 14 preteen. Or wearing gloves at a party because the bottle of polish remover has been long and mysteriously missing. Her new white blouse has been to the laundry three times and she hasn't worn it yet.

These are definite mother-maddeners, not only graphic, but individually entertaining.

Or back to Jane Goodsell's "Women Never Nag!":

> See the unshoveled patio? Look at the broken gate hinges and the shrubs that need staking. Isn't it a shame to leave window screens up all winter? . . . Women would rather paint the downspouts and shingle the roof themselves than run the risk of being naggers.

Or Alan King's "Fit for What?":

> What does my wife do on weekends? I don't know. She acts like she's just won Strike It Rich. She's out of the house by 7:30 a.m. with her golf clubs, her bowling ball, and my wallet.
>
> I've got to admit that my wife is a pretty good housekeeper. . . . Come over sometime and look in my bureau drawers. To get

* From *Good Housekeeping* Magazine (September, 1959). © 1959 by the Hearst Corporation.

a pair of socks, I've got to dig past a sewing box, a roll of wall-paper, a stuffed dog, an electric baseball game, a broken ashtray, last night's newspaper, and last month's unopened bills. When she's finished dusting, even the dustcloth goes into my drawer Two weeks ago, I wore it to work.

By putting a number of quite logical but unlikely objects in such a string, you achieve a comical effect. Everybody's had similar experiences (recognition) but the dissimilarity of the items lends freshness and surprise. Then the artist's touch comes with that supreme hyperbole: "I wore it to work."

The gimmick

One way to organize an article for funniest effect is to present it in a familiar, and logical, but highly unlikely framework. One of the early masters of this was William Hazlett Upson, creator of Alexander Botts, whose letters to and from The Earthworm Tractor Company related his sales exploits, and entertained generations. They first appeared in *The Saturday Evening Post,* and if you study the *Post's* Human Comedy section, you will see how often this device, or others, still serve as vehicles for humor:

"To Heck in a Handcar," by Martin Kitman, is dated "November, 1995" and begins, "Dear Stockholder:" a merry account of what's happened to the railroad industry since Congress gave it liberty "to get out of the unprofitable commuter business."

"Is This Any Way to Run an Airline? (Don't Ask Me)" by Richard Lemon, kids both airlines and poll-takers, with purported questions and answers about their service.

Normand Poirier's "Plead Insanity and Skip Three Turns" uses a Monopoly game:

GO TO JAIL, GO DIRECTLY TO JAIL, DO NOT PASS GO,
DO NOT COLLECT $200

The law isn't that blunt anymore. Card should read: "Go to jail, unless preliminary hearing shows you were improperly advised of Constitutional rights against self-incrimination, in which case, roll again."

GET OUT OF JAIL FREE

Why should anyone get out of jail free? A card reading "The American Civil Liberties Union Defends You Free" would be liberal enough. Or why not just "Plead Insanity." (Insane players should remain immobile for three rolls of the dice.)

A hilarious article by Jack Roche is "The Mother Goose Report," in which the characters have been investigated and are now Cases for the Department of Social Assistance:

Case No. 734—
HORNER, JACK: Boy of indeterminate age. Parents report failure to motivate him toward normal participation in family life. Boy sits constantly in corner with pie. Occasionally sticks thumb in pie, pulls out plum and shouts, "What a good boy am I." Conduct indicates guilt psychosis.

Case No. 723—
JACK AND JILL: Two adolescents prone to accident due to sub-standard housing. Constantly sustain severe contusions when making daily trip up hill to fetch a pail of water. Boy falls down hill. Girl comes tumbling after. Necessity to climb hill for water indicates lack of adequate residential water supply. Recommend referral to Department of Housing and scheduling of daily visits by boy to outpatient clinic for treatment of broken crown.

Such inventiveness on the part of the writer makes his humor leap from the page. And since all humor is really rooted in satire, an original device makes that satire more pungent even as you laugh.

Some general guidelines

Here's a recap of things to aim for and to watch out for in writing humor, plus a few more suggestions:

1. Don't fall back on old gags or typical jokes.
2. Never make less fortunate individuals the butt of your humor.

3. Don't inject humor at the wrong time or in the wrong context.

4. Watch your timing. There must be a brisk, lively beat.

5. Don't substitute hysteria for hyperbole. (Be wary of such verbs as "stamped," "screamed," "bellowed," "whimpered," "moaned," etc.)

6. Watch your tone.

7. Never inject negatives such as: "I know this isn't very funny." (If it isn't, the reader won't have to be told.) Or, in the manner of some TV comedians whom I promptly turn off: "Boy, did that lay an egg," or "Who wrote this terrible script, anyhow?"

8. Never exhort the reader: "Boy, did I laugh," or "It was absolutely rib-splitting," or "Tears of laughter rolled down our cheeks." Humor cannot be described or discussed, it must come from the writing itself.

9. Watch out for *italics,* CAPITAL LETTERS, exclamation points!! Lavish or frantic punctuation cannot compensate for lack of cleverness.

10. Bright or witty effects can be achieved through: Puns. Cliché twists. A play on words. Use of opposites. Specifics.

11. Be very careful of slang and swearing.

Some writers have the impression that a subject is made funny by mere breeziness of style. To achieve this breeziness they lean heavily on slang. Phrases such as, "Man, oh, man—," "Sez who? Sez me," "Oh, yeah?" etc. Or they inject totally meaningless asides intended to convey some mood of humor. "Still do" (make these mistakes), or "still am" (trying to learn better), "Well, you never know," "Could be," "It just goes to show—"

Sometimes, to add to the slam-bang effect, they throw in swearing: "It was really one helluva situation." "What do you do in a case like that, for Chrissake?" Or they sprinkle oaths through the dialogue. Perhaps they do this because they have *heard* some very funny individuals talk that way. But live, "in-person" comedy is always generated as much by the personality of the clown himself as by the things he says. You simply cannot capture this and make it funny on paper. It only gets bombastic, noisy, dull—and is sometimes in bad taste.

12. Don't depend upon things or situations too obviously *expected* to be funny (the antics of a monkey, for instance, a man's bald head, a woman's girdle, losing your undies on the street). The late syndicated columnist George Dixon once wrote a piece on humor in which he said: "The trouble is that the broader the absurdity, the harder it is to make it come out funny on paper" adding that the two principal ingredients of humor are shock and surprise.

This relates right back to two principles of any good creative article: Recognition and surprise. When we go a step further, when the ordinary, the logical, are exaggerated or so twisted about that they become astonishing or highly unusual, then something in the reader responds—he is amused. Thus we achieve humor, whether a piece is funny in its entirety, or merely amusing in spots or in general tone.

10

Twelve Secrets of Style

Style is that elusive element in writing that some people say cannot be taught. Fundamentally, I agree. Like rhythm or good taste or passion, if you have to explain to somebody what it *is,* then don't bother; he probably doesn't have it.

Yet the truly creative writer (and the only one who should try the creative article) *can* be shown definite ways to improve his own style.

Just what *is* style? Whether or not you need the following definition, I want to share my concept of it. This is my definition of style:

> *The art of clear, effective, and readable writing. The rhythm that makes a sentence sound right to the mental ear. The ruthless cutting out of phrases that only clutter and impede this special music. And always, always, the patient, painstaking search for the perfect combination of words and phrases that will create this mental music and express what is to be said in the most moving and effective way.*

Style is important. Of style, Aristotle said, "It is not enough to know what to say; we must also say it in the right way." The first impression an editor gets from any piece of writing is the author's style. The subject may be a good one, the words sufficient—like clothes, they may *cover* it; but if they are sloppy, prosaic or dull, or merely inappropriate, the editor has to drive himself to get through the manuscript.

How to develop style

Any definition of style leaves room for infinite variations. Style is a matter of taste, hence there is no absolute. No one is qualified to say that this, and only this, is the proper way to express anything. The style of some writers is blunt, terse, staccato. The style of others may be brisk, blithe, full of caprice. The style of still others may flow. Sometimes a writer uses one effect so consistently, it is possible to identify his work without a byline.

Most writers vary their style, using some or all of the foregoing effects to suit their material, although generally one style —cadences, individualities of expression—will predominate.

In short, your style is *your* way of writing. Usually it forms slowly over the years, colored by your own maturing and by the subconscious absorbing of words, phrases, meters, expressions, both oral and written. Particularly by the conscious or unconscious imitation of the rhythms and technics of the material you most often read.

Now maturing means not simply growing older, but growing in awareness, in depth, and in our critical faculties. Very often the books which enthralled us in our youth strike us in our middle years as unbelievably bad. Our own early writing efforts now sometimes turn our stomachs. How *could* I have been so inept, so pompous or so wordy? (For this very reason I advise saving everything you write; it will show you how much you have improved.) Again, the truly creative writer often finds some of his earlier work astonishingly good. This, too, is excellent for the ego; it confirms the fact that the talent was always there, and worthy of your continuing labor, determination and sacrifice.

Frequently, a writer's later works don't live up to his first successes. Most critics agree that Thomas Wolfe never equaled his *Look Homeward, Angel;* that Sinclair Lewis was written out before his last books; and I found myself waging a futile struggle to get into Thornton Wilder's *The Eighth Day,* longing for the lucid simplicity of *The Woman of Andros.* But the writer of short forms such as the creative article need not worry about going into a style decline. It is like playing the piano—the more you practice the more effortless and polished your performance will become.

This, then, is a cardinal rule: *You must write!* Not just occasionally, but regularly, if you are to develop style.

Style is also developed through *awareness of the style of others.*

It is no accident that most writers are avid readers. If you are truly creative, reading stirs the spirit of your own creativity. Ideas begin to beat their wings, phrases to sing; you often must stop reading and fly to the typewriter to write. (For this reason, paradoxically, the most prolific writers are not as widely read as many non-writers who aren't inhibited by these interruptions.) When this happens you are generally moved to write in the mood or style of the work that has excited you.

In fact, you can develop certain aspects of your style more quickly and effectively if you will intentionally expose yourself to the kind of things you want to write. If you're going to write humor, steep yourself in humor. Read it particularly just before you sit down to write. The same goes for more thoughtful pieces. Put the subconscious to work, as I suggested in an earlier chapter; let it absorb the mood, the pace, the tone. Then when you get to the typewriter, you are warmed up and ready to go. You'll get off to a faster start and write more fluently and better.

Now this is far different from a conscious imitation of anyone else's style. Read widely in the field of your favorites, instead of reading any single writer too much. Otherwise your work will be "full of echoes." Wolfe imitators only sound like second rate Thomas Wolfes. Or, as Faulkner once told a hopeful who sent him some manuscripts, "Your writing sounds more like me than I do." No, the truly creative writer wants to develop a style that is uniquely his own. Yet every writer of honesty as well as distinction will acknowledge that his style has been influenced by writers before him. And generally it is an amalgam; into the deep well of his subconscious have poured the word patterns of many authors he has admired—no two of them really alike, but all of this fused and forged by the flame of his own genius, to emerge as the style that most suitably expresses the things that his spirit demands.

In developing style, however, one should *consciously take note* of how other good writers achieve their effects. Train yourself to be aware. Mark passages that please you and reread them, searching out why. Underscore good figures of speech, count their frequency and taste their particular flavor. Pay especial attention to rhythms.

For years I schooled myself to read with a deliberate consciousness of rhythms. I remember reading Claire Booth Luce's autobiography and *feeling,* consciously, subconsciously, and emotionally the sure and delicate balance of her phrases. You could almost have measured them with a metronome. "Rhythm!" I wrote on each installment, as I ripped it from the newspaper. "Notice the rhythm." This, I think, is the way anyone who really cares about his own style develops; he is never indifferent to the writing of others. Both consciously and unconsciously he seeks to learn and improve from the best that comes his way.

This approach, together with constant writing practice, is the best possible way to develop your style.

Secrets of style

Let's look now at some specific suggestions for improving style.

1. Be simple. Write so that "all who run may read."
Somerset Maugham said the important elements in writing are "clarity, simplicity, euphony, and liveliness." Clarity and

simplicity, notice. For writing is communication. And certainly in the creative article we must say what we mean in the most direct and simple, if (we hope) engaging way. But this admonition applies to any form of writing.

I do not consider obscurity the mark of profundity. A good mind with a good idea should strive to make that idea understood. When the author chooses instead to bury it in verbiage, convoluted sentences, and references of such erudition that even the erudite get lost, he is not communicating; he is showing off. Or he is camouflaging an idea that wasn't worth all the mental acrobatics.

Rudolph Flesch has a fine time with this sort of thing in his delightful book *The ABC of Style—a Guide to Plain English,* which he also subtitles, "A word diet for the verbally overweight." It is recommended reading, especially for people who have fallen in love with their professional jargon. Jargon has no place in the creative article. Yet when clergymen, educators, government workers, psychologists, etc., attempt articles for mass circulation they often find themselves unwilling or unable to speak the language of laymen. Here, for example, are some excerpts from a would-be article for parents by a woman who teaches child psychology at a large university:

> The adolescent is very anxious to conform to the peer group. When the peer group proposes behavior that may be alien to behavior patterns considered acceptable at home, the adolescent undergoes severe emotional strain. This may be unapparent to parents whose primary objectives are to meet the child's physical and material needs as dictated by their own peer groups, yet who fail to comprehend the child's resultant motivational conflicts as reflected in standards evolving within the framework . . . etc.

Such pedantry is not only straight from Dullsville, it isn't even clear.

To improve your style, let your work cool off a few days after you have it down on paper. Then reread, searching out every sentence that may be fusty, pompous, turgid or too complex;

that does not say exactly what you mean. This does not mean that you cannot be subtle, or artful, or that you must be blunt or "write down." Only that you must be clear. And the more simple and clear you are, the lovelier your writing style will become.

2. Avoid trite phrases and clichés.

Trite phrases or figures of speech are the kiss of death to any manuscript. And that "kiss of death" is exactly what is meant by a cliché: Any group of words that has become hackneyed and stale from overuse.

In the creative article, as in any piece of writing for popular consumption, the style must, of course, sound natural. We use the vernacular, we toss in commonplace phrases, an occasional slang expression, to achieve that quality of "liveliness" Maugham mentioned (as opposed to the textbookish horror cited). But the writer who does this knows what he's doing; he is not leaning on a creaky old cane of clichés because he is mentally too lazy or enfeebled to think of anything better.

A pleasing style is a matter of continuing originality—not freakish, not way out, but a constant inventiveness on the part of the author, who seeks always to present his thoughts in combinations that are fresh, arresting, filled with little surprises. The reader may not be aware of this at all; he may not have the slightest idea why one writer charms him, another does not. It is just one of those subtle secrets of style that the accomplished writer masters through practice and observation (along with his own talent) and then forgets he's using.

The very first step in achieving this inventiveness is to go through every manuscript, ruthlessly cutting every obvious cliché.

Figures of speech such as: "a carpet of grass," "cool as a cucumber," "rich as Croesus," "light as a feather, soft as butter, hard as nails." The time-weary adage, epigram, phrase or quotation: "Ours not to reason why, ours but to do or die." "Man cannot live by bread alone." "While there's life there's

hope." "Man brings home the bacon." Any combinations of
words that are trite: "The day of reckoning," "staunch friend,"
"careworn hands," "face facts," "call a spade a spade," "cry
from the rooftops."

An *occasional* use of common figures and phrases may
lend just the homely, forthright touch you need, and it's impossible to avoid them altogether; but generally speaking they
should be avoided.

A sure cure for clichés is to put them to work for you. Twist
them around, change even *one word,* and the phrase will have
the ring of familiarity while producing surprise.

Here's how it works with similes and metaphors: "Dry as a
rope," Robert Knowlton uses in one of his *Good Housekeeping*
stories—and we snap to attention. A rope *is* dry, and far livelier
than the dreary old "bone" a lazier writer would have settled
for. "Cool as a popsicle" is more colorful than "cool as a cucumber." And instead of a carpet of grass, have the yard wear
a "miniskirt of grass." Or make it "a wall-to-wall carpet of
grass—the neighbor's wall and ours."

Or change one word in any familiar saying: "Man cannot live
by martinis alone," quipped Ramsey Clark at a Press Club
dinner. "You need this advice like you need a hole in your typewriter," a friend told me yesterday.

Or twist the tail of your cliché for a double effect: "Man
may bring home the bacon, but his wife still has to cook it." In
a light article I did about women's spending habits: "Ours not
to reason why, ours but to buy and buy."

You can juggle clichés into clever titles: "The *Un*sound and
the Fury" (H. Allen Smith); "I Must Go Down to the Beach
Again, *Must* I?" (John Skow); "Man's Worst Friend" (Pam-
ela Gordon); "The Dye Is Cast" and "*Don't* You Be My
Valentine" (two of mine).

The unwitting use of clichés is the mark of the amateur; the
professional uses them only deliberately.

3. Make your figures of speech appropriate.

Figures of speech, like anecdotes, are a natural, almost inescapable form of human discourse. Listen to any speaker, in public or private, and the comparisons pop out: "She's a big cow of a woman." "Marriage is like a superhighway: once you get on it's sometimes impossible to get off." "Now take this clock; if I were to break it and try to put it back together I'd have the same kind of mess we're facing now—" "The cartilage between these vertebrae is tough but soft—like a sausage, or a cushion." People talk this way all the time, even prosaic people; it's one way to make ourselves understood. And the more colorful the person, the more colorful and apt his comparisons usually are.

When it comes to writing, there are authors who develop an excellent style without ever using figures of speech. But for most creative writers, imagery—new similes and metaphors—is a source of pleasure and will add not only color to the script, but also clarity. And when such figures of speech are appropriate to the background material, they intensify that material, tie the whole piece neatly together, and add cohesiveness.

A good example of this is found in an excellent article, "Don't Knock the American System to Me," by ex-jobs corpsman and world heavyweight champion George Foreman, in *Nation's Business*. "In my business, boxing, I know a lot about giving hard knocks and getting them too. . . . But knocking the American system, that I can't take." By using the metaphors of his own profession, he drives home the point that anybody can make good if he's willing to "fight" for his dreams. "Battles have to be taken on alone." He says of President Johnson: "The whole country kind of had him on the ropes. . . . He'd made the big decision not to be their punching bag any more."

Another example of appropriate figures of speech is in James Stewart Gordon's characterization of his ski instructor: "A wispy snowflake of a man . . . with muscles like the cables of a ski lift." These figures are definitely appropriate to a wintry mountainside setting and to the man's job, whereas illogical figures would have been comparing him to an African gazelle, say, or his muscles to jungle vines.

To illustrate this from some of my own articles and stories: An architect sees the sky as a vast blueprint, the trees as the strong timbers of a building. To an interior decorator hills are "upholstered in the gaudy colors of autumn." To a seamstress the spring earth is "needlepointed in fine little stitches of green." Rain does not dance on a roof for a stenographer, to her it is typing; it would be tap-dancing if the character or background were a dancing studio. In an article about garden clubs I referred to "a bouncing bouquet of women whose own petals might be fading, but whose stems were still sturdy and whose roots were green." I used verbs like "pluck, cut, dig, gather achievements in a basket." "Enthusiasm runs dry and has to be watered."

By using a little free association, you will find some delightful figures will present themselves to you. And when figures of speech are drawn directly from the background material, they accomplish three things: Give unity to the article. Emphasize your point. Add sparkle to your style.

4. Don't mix figures of speech.

Better no images at all than mixed ones. This does not mean that you must use only one figure of speech, even in variation, throughout the article or story. That would be monotonous. What I mean is that they should be in reasonable harmony with the subject, the background, and each other, and that two or more cannot be allowed to fight it out in the same sentence or paragraph.

Here is a grim example: "These rules and regulations, which seemed at first to be an open gate to freedom, would soon boomerang into a leering monster." In the first place, rules by their very nature are restricting; the *last* thing they normally would suggest is an open gate. But even if they did somehow represent a gate, that gate could not boomerang, and that boomerang could not become a monster. Here we have three totally divergent images, as unalike as possible, and the result is not only bad writing, it is nonsense. It confuses instead of clarifying.

5. Avoid rare, difficult words (but don't throw your thesaurus away).

Obscurity is not, I repeat, a sign of erudition. And the deliberate use of long mouthfilling words calculated to impress the reader, is more likely to irritate him. When I wrote my first novel I was very eager to sound like a cross between T. S. Eliot and Thomas Wolfe. Accordingly, I cluttered it up with remote classical references and never used a simple word where a blockbuster would do. Good editing eliminated most of this, but a few remained, and I remember being actually flattered when one of the most learned women in Pittsburgh called me to say she had consulted all her dictionaries and still couldn't find a certain word. I should have been ashamed.

On the other hand, there is simply no excuse for being word poor. Your dictionary and your thesaurus offer a dazzling banquet of words, all free, all yours. And the truly creative writer is or should be a word hound, hungry for more. "That's a good word," you'll hear him exclaim in conversation, "why don't I use that more often?" Not a rare or unusual word necessarily, but merely a *good* word that has somehow failed to make itself at home in his general vocabulary.

6. Seek always for the right, the perfect word.

The truly creative writer cares deeply about words—enough to take infinite pains to make his writing style as nearly perfect as possible. This means a constant quest to find the one word that most precisely expresses his thought. Here his thesaurus is invaluable. He knows that somewhere in it lurks that word. Occasionally he is baffled, he fails to find it. In order to proceed he may have to substitute; even so, consciously and subconsciously his mind continues its quest until suddenly, in the middle of the night perhaps, the right word soars to the surface.

Good writing can come only from this quality of deep caring, and this willingness to work toward perfection. Bad writing comes sometimes less from lack of talent than from sheer carelessness. You have to know what a word really *means* before you can use it properly. Yet many would-be writers snatch at a word that reasonably resembles the one they think they want. The result is like the singer who doesn't quite hit the note. So suddenly and unexpectedly sour, it can be hilarious. Or it's like the person whose dialogue is entertaining because of its comical near-misses. We once had a laundry man whose weekly appearance I eagerly anticipated because of remarks like this: "The house was absolutely *infatuated* with bedbugs!" . . . "We always wanted children but my wife had a misconception."

7. Don't repeat key words (unless for emphasis or effect).

Two glaring signs of the amateur are the prevalence of clichés, and word repetitions. The first thing I do in criticizing is to mark them on the script. Any good editor preparing a work for publication will do the same.

Let's take care of the opposition first, and acknowledge that some editors disagree about repetitions. I once heard a well-known children's editor pooh-pooh this by showing how Lincoln used repetition in the Gettysburg Address. "Suppose he had said: 'But in a larger sense we cannot dedicate, we must not consecrate, we are unable to hallow this ground. The brave men, living and deceased who passed away here, have immortalized it far above our poor powers—' Isn't that ridiculous?" she concluded.

It certainly was, because the analogy itself was off base. Lincoln, that master stylist, knew exactly what he was up to. He was *intentionally* using repetition for cadence and emphasis. This is very different from using the same word over and over because the author is so mentally impoverished or so lazy that he can't produce a synonym.

I wonder if the editor wouldn't have found it worse if the author of that monumental document had phrased it like this:

"I cannot tell you how moved I am to come here and try to dedicate this ground. As I moved toward this ground and tried to think how to dedicate it I realized that I had dedicated myself to a task which cannot be done. This ground was already dedicated, I thought, by the death of the men who died—"

I had to labor to bring forth that many repetitions in a paragraph but some beginners actually write that way, generally without realizing it. Also some writers who are making progress, still seem absolutely blind to their constant repetitions. I once rewrote a book for a talented woman with a great life story to tell. But that story had been hopelessly entangled in bad organization and verbiage, some of the latter very nice indeed, but most of it cliché-riddled and swamp deep in repetition.

For instance, she would use a certain word, like *wall* incessantly. There were walls between people, stone walls of resistance, walls to build, walls to be chipped away. *World* was another overused word: the world of the mentally ill, private worlds, worlds to learn, worlds to conquer. Week after week I would tear down those "walls" and try to find substitutes for those "worlds" and urge, "Don't repeat!" And when the next chapter came back it too would be heavy with walls, worlds, and other key words which kept bumping into each other, often in the same sentences. Either such people have an idea that individual style is something you're stuck with and can't or shouldn't be improved, or they are quite literally incapable of seeing—or hearing—their faults.

All of us have blind spots when it comes to repetitions. I always let my work cool off, then go over it carefully to find them. But they are like printer's errors: no matter how diligently you read proof, to your dismay they still pop up. One *Reader's Digest* editor has said that this comes about because the mind, having just presented you with a satisfactory word, feeds it right back to you again, and you snatch it and race on unaware of it. If you are pleased with the total effect, your mind may not register the repeated word even on rereading.

But the conscientious writer *cares* about his style sufficiently to stop the offender if he can. I remember once waking in the middle of the night to realize that I had used "shelter" on two successive pages. The next day I called the editor, had her get out the script and change the second to "protection" which was equally descriptive.

If the repetition is used *intentionally* to achieve emphasis or cadence, it is legitimate. Lincoln knew this. It is the careless, unnecessary repetitions that clutter your style and that editors deplore.

8. Watch out for redundancy.

Here is another big offender. A redundancy in basic argument is simply belaboring the obvious, repeating the point needlessly. A redundancy in style uses two words or statements of the same meaning together in sentences or paragraphs:

"The children could cross the street safely and not get hurt."

"Evidently the ostensible purpose was—"

"He was a short fat man, quite heavy and overweight."

9. Discover alliteration

Alliteration adds flow and loveliness to style. It makes your writing sparkle, it smooths the rough edges, it causes a page to perk up, a sentence to sing. Alliteration comes naturally to some writers, others seem totally unaware of it. Yet it is so simple a device for achieving harmony and grace in writing that I marvel more people don't utilize it.

Like anything else, alliteration must be applied with a deft and careful hand. Overdo it and you're dead: "The light leaped nimbly over the limpid lake." "They jumped to the conclusion that just to join would be to get justice." Alliteration does not mean tongue-twisters or fancy frills. Nor is it merely the dumb thump of words that contain the same syllables: "It will be apparent to the parents." "The man was confounded when he found the wallet." "I don't understand how he stands it."

Rather, alliteration is a combination of words that may or

may not begin with the same letter, but whose sounds echo each other, sometimes in the body of the word. And to be truly pleasing, good alliteration joins hands with rhythm. Let's see which is more effective in the following examples:

In *Raintree County,* Ross Lockridge says: "A mile and a half southeast of the lake, the courthouse stood in a lawn of slender trees. A flag fluttered from the brave brick tower, and four clock faces told the time of day."

In the original, there are four "l" sounds in the first sentence: mi*l*e, *l*ake, *l*awn, s*l*ender; which are followed by three in the second: f*l*ag, f*l*uttered, c*l*ock, to*l*d. In the same portion there are six "s" sounds: *s*outhea*s*t, hou*s*e, *s*tood, *s*lender, tree*s*.

In the second sentence the *f*'s predominate: *f*lag, *f*luttered, *f*our, *f*aces. But the *b*'s and *t*'s move in musically: *b*rave *b*rick *t*ower, *t*old, *t*ime.

If we take out the alliteration we also remove most of the melody: "The courthouse was near the lake. There were grass and trees in the yard. It had a brick tower with a flag and a clock."

This is not to suggest that an artist like Lockridge would analyze his own writing as we're doing. But he probably rewrote the original passage, plucking and replucking the strings of alliteration until it brought the most pleasure to him.

Let alliteration go to work for you. It will help to resolve your title problems. It will smooth out those balky sentences and add a few feathers to your writing wings.

10. Keep sentences as short as possible.

Some sentences demand more length than others. But long sentences tend to become involved, convoluted, complex. Study all your sentences carefully to make sure they cannot be improved through shortening. Delete unnecessary phrases. Or break the sentence up. Remember that readability depends a lot upon simplicity. And style, particularly in the creative article, must above all be readable.

11. Develop your inner ear for rhythm.

Read both with your eye and your inner ear. The writer who is conscious of style does this continually, mentally measuring the cadences of writers, registering the variations they employ.

Here are some article openings that I have saved for years because of the sheer rhythmic charm of their style:

"Youth, they say, lives for the future, old age in the past. And the middle years? I do myself doubt whether youth takes more account of the future than can be colored by the mood of a day." ("Mental Annuity" by Elizabeth Bowen, in *Vogue*.) Or Constance Foster's "If I Had a Daughter I'd Tell Her This" in *Ladies' Home Journal*: "They told me, the old ones did when I was young, that childbearing was a sorrow and a pain."

Because of my own aesthetic makeup, sentences like that touch me emotionally and send me into a kind of spiritual waltz. I like their *beat*. You may enjoy cadences of a totally different kind. Very well, note them, mark them, clip them, read them aloud. In so doing you will be making a small but deep impression upon your writing style.

12. Don't be afraid to be original. Give your writing wings!

The truly creative writer of articles or anything else, cannot bear to be just like anybody else. Like Daedalus, he has a positive compulsion to fashion wings of his own and fly. And it is this quality of originality that sends him soaring above the ordinary. In several senses of the word, he gives not only himself but his editor and reader a lift.

This does not mean that you should strain and struggle to be cute or shocking or freakish. Only that you will not settle for the hackneyed, the mundane. Scan every page of every manuscript asking: How can I say this in a better way? Where can I add a bit of stardust, make it sparkle, make it shine? Sometimes you can't, the material itself has so much to do with style. But no matter how serious your message, you do *not* need to sound dull, sluggish, thick-tongued, tired. If you do, you are simply in the wrong business. Certainly you should not try the creative article.

How to achieve this originality? Like style itself, originality is a matter of talent and instinct; unless you have a dash of it within you it cannot really be taught. But there are ways whereby your native gifts can be enhanced and your attitudes improved. As I've already suggested, turn your clichés around (you can do this even in serious articles sometimes). You can do more with alliteration. You can create fresh figures of speech. You can even invent new words. (Mrs. Luce gave us "Globaloney." I have a squib in my column called "Sophistikids," another, "Epigems.") The more you write, the more ways you will discover to put the touch of individuality upon your writing, to give it wings.

Style, your style, *can* be improved. And once you reach the point of caring very much indeed about your style, you will enjoy the act of writing. You will feel the almost sensual pleasure that comes from creating effects with words.

11

Methods and Markets

I would like to share some of my own methods of writing and selling these articles. Also, to answer a lot of random questions that are hurled at me during teaching sessions. The answers may or may not match those that another writer might give. But this is how writing, and selling, the creative article works for me.

The actual writing

1. *Do you outline?*

Only in the sense of putting on paper every idea pertinent to the subject that occurs to me. This may include whole passages or paragraphs that may be used, or merely fragments, phrases, suggested thoughts or approaches. This outline, if you can call it that, goes into a Manila folder, where supplementary material can be tossed.

The folder, labeled with a tentative title, is filed, alphabetically, where I can find it easily.

I have learned to use good strong paper for this outline (or for anything used in notebook or journal) rather than cheap yellow second sheets which wear out easily (your notes may age a long time before you need them); also to write on only one side of the paper. If you try to put down on the back ideas for other articles, you can't file properly, and even ideas pertinent to this particular article may be forgotten or lost.

2. *When is the best time to actually write the article?*

When you're excited about it. Thus the rough outline you start may grow into the completed manuscript before the day is over. Or it may have to wait until a new and urgent style or approach occurs to you.

I think it is a good idea to write as much of the actual article as you can at the first sitting, but never in the sense of, "I am now writing an article." Rather, "I'm just roughing this one out." You'll write more freely, and cover lots more territory. Then later, when you think, "I shall now write that article," you will find that a lot of the work has been done. It now may be only a matter of organizing more carefully, and polishing.

3. *How long should these articles be?*

From 1500–2500 words. As the preacher said, "Be there. Be brief. Be gone."

4. *What about illustrations?*

You don't have anything to do with them.

5. *How should the finished manuscript look?*

Professional. Use a good grade of white paper. Get a good supply of black typing ribbons. *Don't economize on ribbons.* When a ribbon begins to go gray, remove it and save for the rough composition work of every day.

Don't economize on paper either. Leave wide margins, top, bottom, and sides. For your own sanity, don't be stingy with carbon paper—it, too, is relatively cheap, and it's maddening to try to read your own dim copy when the original is out.

In typing, be sure your keys are clean; scrub them with alcohol or use commercial cleaner on ink-clogged ones. Resist overstrikes, and don't ever x out. Avoid pencil corrections. An occasional one doesn't hurt, but messy pencil changes break the reading flow and are irritating. Better to retype.

If the manuscript gets soiled or mail-weary, be sure to retype it. The marks of those abominations, paper clips, can be ironed out. By placing a light cloth or other piece of paper over the page you're ironing, you will avoid a shiny look or curling. Be careful not to get the iron too hot—some papers blister!

6. *How do I mail it?*

Very short pieces, up to 1,000 words, may be folded in thirds and mailed in long white envelopes—with sufficient postage. Longer ones may be folded once in the middle and submitted in 6x9 or 7x10 Manila envelopes, with a piece of cardboard, the same size, inserted. It is the usual custom for pieces 2000–2500 words or more to be mailed flat in a big Manila envelope, again with cardboard inserted.

Always enclose a stamped, self-addressed envelope, rather than loose postage. Invest in a small postal scale to weigh your offering going and coming, and be sure to use enough postage.

5. *When do you send it out?*

Not until you're sure you've made the manuscript as perfect as possible. It's best to wait a few days, then reread to catch typing errors or little things you may have missed before. Sometimes a few passages have to be rewritten—perhaps only a lead or an ending. Invariably there is something that needs touching up before you mail it.

If the article is seasonal, submit it at least four months before the target date.

6. *Do I copyright my article?*

Articles may not be copyrighted prior to publication. To put a copyright notice on your manuscript (it is meaningless) is the mark of an amateur. When an article is published, it will be protected by the copyright covering the entire issue of the publication where it appears. A book contract should provide for the copyright to be taken out in the author's name.

7. *What about rights?*

Some magazines buy all rights, but most will then reassign the secondary rights to you and send you a check, if a reprint magazine should use your article.

Marketing

1. *Where do I submit my creative article?*

To the most appropriate magazine—in other words, one which uses this type of article and would be likely to be interested in the subject you have chosen.

Before you write it, you should have one, or several, magazines in mind. I think it's best to start at the top, with the big circulation magazines, even though the competition for their rates is keen. Big magazines *are* open to good work from newcomers. In addition to their major sections, some have departments especially receptive to contributions from their readers.

And the old saw is true—aim at the stars if you would hit the trees. Thus, if the stars reject you, you have a whole grove of trees lined up—in other words, lesser markets.

2. *How do I find out what these are?*

By studying the writers' magazines and markets. In addition to the big-circulation magazines listed, you will find literally hundreds of less well-known outlets, some of which use the creative article. These include religious and inspirational magazines, newspaper supplements, smaller women's magazines, lodge journals, and even some trade journals. (Edith Hunter's "The Grand Opening That Didn't" appeared first in *Petroleum Today* before being reprinted in *Reader's Digest*.)

Second, by studying the magazines themselves. Browse on supermarket newsstands while waiting in line at the check-out counter. Use your time in the doctor's waiting room. Ask friends to save their magazines of special interest. Get religious publications from friends of different denominations; fraternal magazines like *Elks* and *The Rotarian*, from members; pick up *Ford Times, Buick*, etc., from dealers. Don't overlook the reading racks in churches, or places of business. The art-of-living booklets there provide another market for your article, either as a reprint or an original.

Study all these publications for total content and tone. Then, when you find a good creative article, analyze *it*, to see what made it acceptable.

I cannot emphasize too strongly the importance of trying these other fields if you really wish to place your work. I have had students who were on the verge of giving up when they discovered them and began to sell.

3. *How do you analyze published articles?*

Mark and clip! Read with pencil and razor blade. In marking, note the lead, and how often it is tied into the final paragraph. I mark *A* for Anecdote in the margin, and frequently count these anecdotes—A.#1, A.#2, A.#3—etc. *D* is for discussion. *Q* for quotes. If a memory device or symbol is used, I note it. If the style is particularly pleasing, I write an enthusiastic: STYLE! across the top. Apt figures of speech should also be underscored.

The writer who really wants to improve is his own best teacher. And his texts are these published pieces that he wants to emulate.

4. *Is a query letter necessary before submitting articles?*

The creative article is so subjective that this is a hard question to answer. If the manuscript runs over 1500 words, yes, I think you should query. Anything under that is really not worth the effort. On very short articles, 1000–1500 words, write the entire piece and submit it. Selling these idea pieces depends so much on style and actual treatment, most editors prefer seeing the whole thing.

On the longer ones, 2,000 words or more, a query is in order, as you will be going into the subject more deeply, using more references. It gives the editor a chance to tell you if he already has something of that nature in the works, and can save you effort.

5. *How do you prepare a query letter?*

State the title and idea immediately, giving a sample treatment of the type you will be using in the opening paragraph.

Then summarize the general contents of the proposed article. Give your qualifications for writing it, and the approximate word length. Stop.

For example:

Dear Mr. James:
Winston Churchill once said, "I'd rather face a lion unarmed at twenty paces, than listen to a lady speaker." A lot of people would agree with him. Speeches by ladies can be pretty ghastly experiences—for both lady and listener. That's why I'm interested in doing an article:

BEFORE YOU GO ON THE PLATFORM, LADY

in which I offer some suggestions that should make the experience a lot more pleasant for both. In it I wish to discuss both Preparation and Presentation, from a number of angles—including voice and dress. I have quotes from a number of authorities—Cornelia Otis Skinner, Hester Provenson, who conducts courses in speech and protocol in Washington, D.C., and others. I have also done a great deal of lecturing myself.

My work has appeared in a number of magazines, including _____, _____, _____. I could write to length, but think 2,000 words would be about right for this article. I believe it would appeal to your audience.

Thank you for your consideration.
                                        Sincerely,

If your work has *not* appeared in any magazines, just leave that line out. *Don't* list a lot of magazines the editor may never have heard of—just say your work has appeared in a number of magazines, but don't specify. *Don't* inform him that you are President of a writer's club and this article has just won a prize in your annual contest. (No editor is ever impressed by the acclaim of amateurs.)

6. *To whom should this letter, or the article itself, be addressed?*

To the Managing Editor, by name, as listed on the masthead, or to the Articles Editor, also by name, if listed, or to some appropriate subordinate editor. These lesser editors receive less mail than their superiors, and are more likely to pay attention to you. Also, it's to their credit when they bring in an acceptable piece of work.

7. *Do I need an agent?*

Reputable agents won't bother with articles by beginners or pieces that don't bring in big payments. When an agent sells an article for you for $500.00, his commission (10%) is only $50.00. And if you are willing to sell an article to a small magazine for $25.00, an agent's commission would come to only $2.50, hardly worth his while.

My best advice to beginners is to send these highly subjective ("creative") articles out on their own and hope for the best. If you should make some big sales, agents will be asking you to let them have a chance at selling your work.

How to get along with editors

1. Submit only clean, double-spaced *original* copy on good white paper. (Never colored paper or onion skin.) Never submit carbons or photocopies.

2. Submit only one manuscript at a time. (A group of two or three very short sketches would be acceptable, however.) Never deluge an editor with a collection of rejects or even new articles. Let him give his undivided attention (you hope) to one article, before rejecting or accepting it.

3. If querying, submit only one *idea* for a proposed article at a time. "Never give an editor his choice of several," a very fine editor once told me. "In picking one he's automatically turning down the others, remember. Try him on each, one at a time."

4. Send only material that is appropriate to the magazine. This is mere good marketing sense. An article on weaning a baby could scarcely find a place in *Popular Mechanics,* or the

story of how you saved your marriage in *Holiday*. Yet some writers bombard the markets blindly, without bothering to find out what they could conceivably use. This not only wastes your time and postage, it irritates the very busy people who have to return all this hopelessly inappropriate material.

By "appropriate," we mean material that has *some* relationship to the contents of the magazine. This is where the ability to slant and to aim with good judgment can help you to place articles. *Petroleum Today* would seem a very unlikely market for Edith Hunter's lovely "The Grand Opening That Didn't," referred to earlier. But this creative article about a little boy's learning the secrets of nature *was* appropriate because of its direct relationship to the magazine's theme: The youngster was playing service station; he used discarded oil cans and old spark plugs, hub caps, inner tubes, in which the robins and rabbits came to nest. Undoubtedly the editors welcomed this as a charming (but appropriate!) change of pace; *Petroleum Today* published it and it was also condensed in *Reader's Digest*.

I have had many writing students who began to sell regularly, once they made a real study of the markets, particularly the smaller ones, and began to slant their creative articles to the market needs. Editors appreciate writers who show this kind of judgment.

Such writers know their markets, and what is appropriate for them. Editors appreciate writers who show this kind of judgment.

5. A brief letter citing the article by title and identifying yourself is good practice, although I have sold many articles cold, without an accompanying line. If you do write a letter, *don't* do any of the following:

Don't ask the editor what his needs are; you're supposed to know.

Don't ask for a free sample copy at the time you submit

your manuscript. Get one first and study it. Better yet, borrow or buy one if it's on the newsstands.

Don't ask for advice or criticism.

Don't say you're just a beginner and will sell cheap, or even let him have the work for nothing. (Nobody should be that desperate.)

Don't put a price on your work. In fact, say nothing about payment. The magazine has its rates, and if your article is accepted, you will be paid accordingly.

Don't tell the editor your life story. Especially your problems—how the house just burned down, your husband has eloped with a belly dancer, leaving you with the sole support of nine children, and one of them has polio. Editors are not social workers; their job is to find and pay for acceptable material.

6. Don't pester an editor for reports.

Many magazines are infernally slow; this you have to accept. A delay may mean that they are simply swamped and have not had time to consider your contribution. Or it may mean that they are seriously considering it and need more time to make up their minds. The best thing to do is to have so much material in the mail that you don't waste your own time worrying about the fate of a single piece.

However, a courteous prod after six or eight weeks is O.K. —"According to my records, my article, 'Dare To Be Different,' was submitted to *Up and Coming* on January 21. I wonder if it reached you safely, and if you have come to a decision concerning it." Suffering in silence may be noble, but manuscripts do sometimes get lost in the mail, or behind a secretary's desk.

7. Don't accuse editors of stealing your ideas.

People in the publishing business are not crooks. If a magazine should publish something similar after turning your article down, theirs was probably in the file long before yours showed up. Or they may have received a much better article on the same subject later.

Sometimes a staff writer is assigned to work with or for an

amateur whose idea is too good to turn down, but again whose presentation is poor. In this case, the original author is always consulted and paid.

The writer must operate on faith, as we must in other areas of life. The last thing he can afford to do is to develop an attitude of skepticism and suspicion in relation to editors and publishers.

8. Never send in a manuscript that an editor has already rejected—unless you call his attention to that fact, and have some very good reason, such as a revision, to ask him to reconsider. If you have exhausted all your markets and feel that you must start over, rewrite the article and tell the editor why you think it's now more appropriate to his needs. (The magazine itself may have undergone a change of policy.) Otherwise forget it until the editor moves, or dies.

9. Be friendly but businesslike. This is just as important after you've sold an editor as it is before. In the first blush of acceptance, you may love him madly and imagine the feeling is mutual. Just remember he's dealing with a lot of other authors too.

It is desirable to get to New York—or the city of publication wherever it is—and meet editors in person. But *not* until you have sold to them, and have other articles to discuss. Editors just don't have the time or energy to interview hopefuls, however promising. "Sell me something, then come see me," is the attitude they almost have to take. Once this happy circumstance occurs, you may discover that you have interests in common, and in time a genuine friendship may develop. This bond between editor and author is one of the rewards of the writing profession.

But in the beginning at least, it is always firmly rooted on one thing: Your product geared to his needs. A friendly professionalism.

12

How to Become a
Professional

How does the writer of creative articles (or anything else) become a professional?

This question is asked so often that I feel impelled to discuss it here: It seems to me that the amateur becomes a professional when he stops *thinking* of himself as an amateur, and regards himself as a serious, dedicated worker in a highly competitive profession. Only in so doing can he develop the professional working habits that he must have in order to succeed.

This means undergoing some severe emotional spasms that may not seem professional in themselves: the longing to write at inconvenient times; the maddening interruptions when you start; the agonizing battle against procrastination; the shock of having your best pieces sometimes go begging; the hours of self-doubt and despair. Or the contrasting ecstasy when you succeed, and it seems for a little while at least that all doors will be open to you for evermore. Also, there are times when you are feted, applauded, made to feel a real celebrity (while a little voice inside you scoffs, knowing the real you so wretchedly well); times when total strangers make a fuss over you—while some of your best friends (you thought) pointedly ignore the fact that you have done anything remotely worthy of notice.

These things constitute just some of the blood, sweat and rejection slips that a real writer must experience on the road to becoming a professional—and thereafter—because, though they let up after a while, or possibly because you are inured to them, for very few people indeed does there ever arrive a halcyon time when all obstacles and difficulties actually stop.

The writer who refuses to be an amateur develops moral muscles—sheer stubborn determination, guts. He manages to go on working in the face of repeated failures. He develops, above all, self-discipline, the discipline that says "No!" to the thousand things that would tempt him, or seemingly force him away from his typewriter. The discipline that must be practiced and mastered if he is to develop professional working habits and become, in the genuine sense, a professional himself.

Procrastination

Procrastination is the beginning writer's—or amateur's— enemy; habit is his ally., because, once you have become the incurable professional, habit will keep you from procrastinating. "We write," as Thomas Wolfe said, "because we want to write so damn bad." By then we not only want so intensely to write, we *are* writing so constantly that habit drives us to the daily rendezvous, almost against our will sometimes.

For the writer who is not yet thus shackled, procrastination takes many forms. The excuses it makes for you are vast and varied. Major among them are your responsibilities to other people. If you are a man, you must support your family, and it's doubtful indeed if you can do it at the typewriter alone. Then, when you get home from your job (sometimes a desk job, a writing job that drains you mentally), it's not only hell to try to write creatively, you figure it's just not fair to shut yourself away from the family. I could not be more sympathetic. It seems to me that *any*body who puts in a full day working at something else has a double handicap. Yet good men do it all the time.

Most families are surprisingly cooperative, once they realize the head of the house is in earnest. They are proud of him and glad for the extra money. They are the last people who would want to be used as excuses for his *not* writing.

Then there are the women with young children. Now *there* is the first-prize, blue-ribbon alibi for postponement. And the world is teeming with frustrated, groaning, non-writing devotees of this particular motherly mystique. They "can't" write with all the duties, problems, demands. Wait until the last one is in school, out of junior high, high school, college, married. But oh dear, now the grandchildren are being parked with you, just when you're getting started! By that time anyway the neglected flower of talent has drooped, wilted, and may never be revived. Worse, the habit of putting it all off until the "right time" arrives is too deeply ingrained to change.

Sooner or later we all must face the fact that the world will never under any circumstances simply stop and let us write.

Even childless people often develop a gift for procrastination that sometimes surpasses that of people with families. They take courses, hold offices in writing clubs, spend hours in libraries doing research, develop impressive filing systems, seek out the company of other writers to discuss ideas, take trips to gather material—do everything but write! *Whereas,* if you have several offspring yelling for attention, such free time as you can wrest from the day is simply too precious to squander. You race to your appointed place at the appointed (or unexpected) hour, and write!

Here are several suggestions:

1. Steer clear of organizations. Let the P. T. A. and the civic circles and luncheon clubs struggle along without you. Join even one and before you know it you're on a committee, or managing a drive. The writer's job is to write!

This must be amended slightly for parents. If you have school-age children, it is not fair to them to ignore the Sunday School picnics and the Cub Scout meetings and other activities that have to do with their normal growing up. Busy writer-parents can and do and must make room for such; but keep your participation at the minimum level that will square with your own conscience and your youngsters' happiness. (But guard that you're not using conscience as an excuse for procrastination.)

After you do become a professional, with the procrastination problem overcome, there are professional organizations which can be a definite help to you. By then the kids will be older and you won't need to feel guilty at foregoing their organizations for those few that prove of definite value to you. You may even allow yourself a day off occasionally just for fun. But in the beginning, don't yield to temptation. Stay home and write!

2. Have your own definite place to work. An office, a study, even a screened-off corner of the bedroom. But somewhere strictly your own where you can go—preferably with a door to shut.

Have a big roomy desk there, and the best equipment you can manage. A good typewriter that you don't have to battle along with everything else. A posture chair. Writing is hard physical work. Make it as comfortable for yourself as you can. When I was having backaches and bouts with bursitis, I invested in a secretarial chair and Underwood's first electric typewriter. The relief was little short of miraculous. Both the typewriter and I are still holding up after more years than I'll admit—and I have not had bursitis since.

Get a filing cabinet, so you don't waste too much time trying to find things. Have bookshelves handy, filled with the books and references you need. Get a second typewriter if you can, a portable to keep in the kitchen or workshop to catch sudden ideas, or to take on trips. And never go *any*where, even overnight, without it. Handwritten notes have a way of getting mislaid or not getting legibly transcribed. Ideas or observations typed on the spot save time and have far more permanent value.

Everything needn't be brand-new; pick up your cabinets and

desk at a fire sale or from a want ad. The main thing is to equip yourself professionally if you are to write professionally.

3. Have a schedule. Write daily at regular hours—early in the morning, or after dinner, if you are employed. Or, if not, during the day between the more predictable activities of the household. Even if your schedule has to be juggled, changed, reshaped as the demands on you alter, the mere fact of *having* a schedule and striving continually to keep it, strengthens that invaluable ally, habit.

4. Get household help, women writers, if you can—at least while the children are pre-school. This is worth almost any sacrifice. Even when it seems as if you're working for *her*, at least you'll be doing work you like.

5. Be patient with interruptions. Do whatever you can to keep them at a minimum, but stop fighting back when they occur. It only wastes valuable emotional energy and time. Spare yourself and everybody else by an attitude of stoic but cheerful acceptance. Then get back to work and do the best you can.

You're licked only when you yield to a frenzied, self-pitying, "It's just no use!"

6. Write every day, whether or not you have an idea, or are "inspired." The sheer act of putting something down on paper will start generating ideas. And quite often the true inspiration occurs during the act of creating, when you are caught up in the process and become excited by what evolves.

Remember this: Habit, the simple act of going to the same place at the same time whenever humanly possible, and doing the same thing there, can save you from procrastination. After a while you will go for no better reason than that you cannot stay away; the strong but subtle hands of habit will draw you there.

Procrastination is the writer's enemy. Habit is his ally.

Clubs, conferences, and critics

Writing is said to be a lonely business. But so is almost any art—and a good thing too. Discussing this, an artist-friend once remarked, "Loneliness is the real beginning of living, the beginning of growth. No artist can ever accomplish anything until he can find out who he really is by working alone." This is especially true of writing. The writer must discover his true capacities by wrestling alone with his own thoughts.

For me this is not loneliness in any self-sacrificing or sad sense. The hours you spend at the typewriter are in the company of so many intriguing characters and ideas that the other form of "loneliness" is suffered more often in the midst of mere mortals who don't share the curious ecstasies and afflictions of writers, or who seem dull by comparison. Yet writers, like most people, love to talk shop, and are thrilled whenever they find other writers who do speak their language. Thus—writers' clubs. And a big bold sign: BEWARE.

Far too many writers' clubs are aggregations of people who like to look, act, and talk like writers, but aren't. Either they don't write enough to qualify, or they don't write well enough to sell. And in spending very much time in their company you are psychologically classifying yourself an amateur, and holding back your own advancement as a professional. Even when they elect you to office, award your work with prizes, and publish it in their journals, they are doing you a disservice, for they are offering a *substitute* for the recognition and payment you should be receiving on the professional playing field.

Another danger of writers' clubs is the criticism generally offered there. The wrong advice from the wrong people can dampen your enthusiasm and confuse you, sometimes fatally. Or it can blow your egotism up out of all proportion to the actual worth of what you have written. Generally speaking, it is a mistake to expose your brain-child to *any*body who is not a bona fide professional. This includes husbands, wives, best friends, as well as fellow hopefuls. There are, of course, exceptions: an unusually brilliant spouse; a club that includes some experienced or truly perceptive people.

But remember the value of loneliness. The true beginning of growth. In the main, your writing should be between you, your manuscript, and its ultimate judge, the editor. Very few professionals ever read or show their unpublished work to anyone else.

How, then, can the beginner learn? He can learn by trial and error, the toughest and in some ways the best teacher. He can also combine and generally cut short some of the trial and error, by taking a good writers' course. Either oral or written, conducted by people who know from experience what they're talking about. Let it be firmly stated here that *no writers' course ever taught anybody how to write. Writers' courses can only take people who already know how to write and teach them how to write better and, hopefully, more successfully.*

These courses need not be expensive. Some excellent ones are available through the adult education programs of high schools and colleges, the YW or YMCA in many cities, and senior citizens' groups. Correspondence courses have the built-in drawback that you may not finish them and get your money's worth. But many inexpensive ones are run by colleges. Some people prefer correspondence courses because of the definite assignments with their written criticisms. But if you have to depend upon assignments or goads of this kind to make you write, you may lack the basic qualifications of talent plus drive that are absolutely essential to ever becoming a professional writer.

Don't keep taking courses. If one, or at the most two, haven't really helped you, forget it.

A good writers' conference can be immensely stimulating. When the workshops, classes and panels are conducted by experienced professionals who are also able to convey know-how and enthusiasm, the time and money couldn't be better spent. But again, don't be a perennial conference-goer. Dive into one or two and soak up all you can. Then go home and *swim,* until you become so proficient on your own that one day they'll be asking you back to teach the next diving class.

The crux of the whole learning process, however, is you, the writer: your talent; your determination to learn, as you can learn by reading, studying, observing, *writing*; your willingness so to arrange your life, at whatever cost, that writing *does* become your real profession. A glorious, exacting, enslaving, freeing, life-enhancing profession at which you work every day, in artistic, emotional, but always professional terms.

The creative article is not the highest form of literary endeavor. It is but *one* form, and a good one, both for the writer and for his reading audience.

If you can write good creative articles, then you may also be able to write other things—short stories, books—works upon which your true achievements as a writer will rest, you hope. Meanwhile you will be receiving the greatest stimulus any writer can have to keep at it—publication in reputable magazines, checks. They may sometimes be small, they may be far apart, but whatever their size or frequency, they are vital signal fires to light the way and help reaffirm your faith in yourself.

Meanwhile, you are also realizing rewards that are equally significant: a chance to share your convictions, your experiences, the lessons you have learned; moments of beauty or inspiration too compelling to keep. And with all this, the knowledge that somewhere out in a chaotic and troubled world somebody is laughing because of you, somebody is kinder, more compassionate, more understanding, more sure of his own dreams or his own strength to carry on.

In writing the creative article you are not only lighting your own often dark paths as a writer, you are lighting the way for other people too.